PASSING YOUR
INSTRUMENT PILOTS
WRITTEN EXAM
2ND EDITION

JEFF W. GRIFFIN

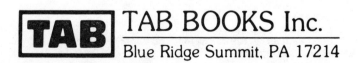

TAB BOOKS Inc.
Blue Ridge Summit, PA 17214

SECOND EDITION

FIRST PRINTING

Copyright © 1985 by TAB BOOKS Inc.

Printed in the United States of America

Reproduction or publication of the content in any manner, without express permission of the publisher, is prohibited. No liability is assumed with respect to the use of the information herein.

Library of Congress Cataloging in Publication Data

Griffin, Jeff.
    Passing your instrument pilot's written exam.

    Includes index.
    1. Instrument flying.   I. Title.
TL711.B6G74   1985   629.132'5214   85-22242
ISBN 0-8306-2385-X (pbk.)

Contents

Acknowledgments

No one arrives at a high point in a career without the help of others. My flying career is totally civilian oriented. That statement is very important. In a highly competitive community such as aviation, to make one's way by the means open to the civilian, without V.A. benefits, is an achievement. Training is expensive. For many, it is out of reach, except for those with desire. If the desire is strong enough, then there are people that will bend over backwards to help you make it. It is those people I wish to thank humbly and sincerely.

It was early in my marriage that I decided to change careers. It was a difficult decision for a guy that already had most of the things that Americans use to measure success. It was even more difficult for my wife, Denise, to accept. Because, in the following three years, we gave up nearly all of our possessions, except a car, to pay for flight training. To her, my deepest gratitude and love.

There were so many people along the way that aided in making my career successful. Many, I can't even recall their names now. You know, the guys that hang around the little grass airports chewing the rag. I listened to them for hours as their hands soared, palms up, through aerobatic maneuvers, and chased clouds and details that had been embellished to a point larger than life. All of it reinforcing that dream, that desire, that image of what flying is all about, and all the time teaching me lessons that may have even saved my life a time or two.

But it was the guys like Ray Brill, now airport manager in

Gaylord, Michigan, that made the difference. Ray financed me when there wasn't any other way to go. I honestly couldn't have made it without him.

Jerry Griffin is my cousin. He gave me the first aviation job I had. I flight instructed and flew charter for over 1200 hours in the eleven months I worked for him. Therein lays my background for instruction and the appreciation for hard work necessary to make it in aviation.

I have been writing for some years and never thought I'd undertake a book on aviation, let alone be asked to write a second edition. Mostly, I write magazine articles, but Clifford Dossey changed all that. Cliff put me in touch with TAB BOOKS Inc., and to him goes deep thanks for broadening my literary career as well as expanding my financial horizons.

Additionally, I'll like to thank the rest of my family. Mom and Dad, though showing reservations about my career decisions after putting me through college to be a geologist, stood behind me and loaned me money when we needed it.

Finally, I'd like to thank David Mann, my first flight instructor. I hope he likes real estate as well as I enjoy flying.

Introduction

Textbooks are great for learning. You should learn all of the basic information pertinent to the Instrument Written Exam from a good textbook and some of the other sources. Instrument ground schools are also an important and effective way to obtain the information necessary to pass the Instrument Written Exam. Then what is this book about?

This book details some innovative problem-solving methods that have been tried and found to be effective. Accelerated ground instructor courses have become popular in the last few years. These accelerated courses are developed to aid applicants for various ratings in remembering easy ways to solve computer problems and methods to remember extraneous information on Federal Aviation Regulations and ATC procedures.

This book should save you time and money. Many of the instrument students that read this book won't be aviation-career oriented people. Rather, you are more likely to be a businessman, lawyer, or doctor looking to increase the utility of the aircraft that you fly. Because so many professional and working people have little spare time, any short cuts to understanding should be welcome. How fast you can go through this book and grasp the methods will vary. I can honestly say, however, it will save you time and grief in the long run.

For this book to help increase your score to a sure passable figure, you just resolve to use the methods described. Any half measures or adaption to your own problem-solving methods will only dilute the effectiveness of these methods.

The various areas of aeronautical knowledge that are covered by the written exam are detailed in each chapter. In the chapters that involve use of a flight computer or a calculator, various formulas are presented. In the last chapter of the book, a formula sheet will be presented. This formula sheet should be memorized as it appears, because everyone has a photographic memory. If the lines and formulas are memorized by their position on the page, it is easier to recall. The idea here is that you can reproduce the formula sheet in the test room. Legally! For your own private use. It is almost like cheating, but better.

Some of the material in this book, especially on FARs, is not numerically oriented. In this instance, memory becomes more difficult. In these cases, where it is possible, I use "catch" phrases. Phrases that will click whenever the subject matter arises in a question.

Chapter one details the material from which the FAA draws its questions. Every applicant should try to read this material. The purpose of this book is to make the exam easier and yield a higher score, not to short cut information. As a flight instructor, I feel it is tremendously important to know everything. After all, shooting a 200 and 1/2 approach with your radios out is not the time to wonder what to do next. It does happen and can happen. Follow the methods outlined in the succeeding chapters and your pass on the first attempt is assured.

Chapter 1

The Test

The Federal Aviation Administration (FAA) uses a question book to determine the aeronautical knowledge of aspiring pilot applicants for the instrument rating. This book contains 800 to 1,000 questions covering three separate airman ratings. Those ratings are the Instrument Airplane, Instrument Helicopter, and the Instrument Foreign Pilot. Although there are over 1,000 questions in the test booklets, each applicant is given a "Question Selection Sheet" and is asked to answer 80 of these questions. The test questions pertain to the Federal Aviation Regulations (FARs). Part 61 deals with Pilot Certification and Part 91 with Operational and Flight Rules, as well as preflight, departure, enroute, and arrival Instrument Flight Regulations (IFR) situations.

Although most of us take one written test or the other, it is possible to hold both the Instrument Airplane and Instrument Helicopter ratings. In the event that one is already certified by the FAA in one of those categories, an applicant need only take a "difference" test. For instance, if you have an Instrument Helicopter rating, all that is required to add an Instrument Airplane rating to your certificate is to take a 15-question test. This short test will pertain specifically to a helicopter or an airplane (depending on the rating you seek) in the areas of performance, weight and balance, weather minimums, and recency of experience. It should be noted that in either case an appropriate flight check is necessary to complete the rating and certify the airman fully.

Table 1-1. Written Test Subject Matter Outline.

Reference code:

AC	—Advisory Circular
AW	—Aviation Weather (AC 00–6A)
AWS	—Aviation Weather Services (AC 00–45A)
AIM	—Airman's Information Manual
EOG	—IFR Exam-O-Gram
IFH	—Instrument Flying Handbook (AC 61–27B)
BHH	—Basic Helicopter Handbook (AC 61–13A)
IAPC	—Instrument Approach Procedure Charts
PHB	—Pilot's Handbook of Aeronautical Knowledge (AC 61–23B)

(FAR references will be indicated by Part number only;
i.e., 91.5 means FAR 91.5.)

FLIGHT PLANNING

A10 **Certificates and Ratings**

    A11 Requirements for certificates and ratings (61.3)

    A12 Eligibility for instrument rating (61.65)

    A13 Where instrument rating required (61.3(e), 91.97)

    A14 Recency of experience (61.57)

A20 **Preflight Action for Flight**

    A21 Familiarization with all available information (91.5; EOG–31; AIM–3)

    A22 Fuel requirements (91.23)

A30 **Preflight Action for Aircraft (EOG–31)**

    A31 Responsibility for airworthiness (91.29)

    A32 Equipment required
          Instruments and equipment (91.33)
          Transponder (91.24, 91.90)
          ELT (91.52)

    A33 Tests and inspections
          VOR (91.25; EOG–22; AIM 1–2)
          Altimeter system (91.170)
          Transponder (91.177)

    A34 Portable electronic devices (91.19)

A40 **Flight Plan (AM—1)**

    A41 When required (91.97, 91.115)

    A42 Information required (91.83)

    A43 Alternate airport requirements (91.83; EOG–29)

B10 Route Planning

B11 Preferred route (AIM–3) ; SIDs and STARs (AIM–1, see Index)

B12 Airport/Facility Directory (AIM–3)

B13 NOTAM (AIM–3A)

B14 FDC NOTAMs (AIM–3A)

B15 Special Notices (AIM–3)

B16 Area Navigation Routes (AIM–3)

B17 Direct Routes (AIM–1, Airspace ; FAR 91.119, and 91.121(b))

B18 Restrictions to En Route Nav. Aids (AIM–3)

B19 Substitute Route Structure (EOG–39)

B20 Flight Planning Computer Operations (Ch. XII–IFH)

B21 Wind correction angle-heading

B22 GS

B23 ETE/ETA

B24 Fuel estimates

B30 Aircraft Performance (Aircraft Owner's Handbook; VFR EOG–33; EOG–32; AC 90–14A)

B31 Takeoff distance

B32 Climb performance

B33 Cruise performance (VFR EOG–38)

B34 Fuel flow

B35 Landing performance

B36 Airspeed: IAS, CAS, EAS, TAS (Ch. XII–IFH)

B37 Placards and instrument markings

B38 Hovering

B40 Aircraft Operating Limitations (documents in aircraft, AC 60–6A)

B41 Weight and balance (EOG–21; AC 91–23A)

B42 Instrument limit markings and placards (FAR 91.31)

B43 Maximum safe crosswind (VFR EOG–27)

B44 Turbulence air penetration

B50 Aircraft Systems (Ch. IV—IFH)

B51 Pitot-static system (EOG–10; IFH, page 55)

B52 Vacuum/gyroscopic (EOG–24)

B53 Electric/gyroscopic

B54 Compass

3

The other instrument written exam is for the foreign pilot. If a foreign pilot should want or need a United States certificate with an instrument rating, a written test will be administered covering the same items pertinent to instrument flight as a U.S. citizen would take. The only difference will be the foreign pilot's test will be hand-scored at the office where it is administered.

All other answer sheets are sent to the FAA Aeronautical Center in Oklahoma City, where they are computer-scored. When the computer finds an error or incorrect answer, the deficiency is indicated by a code. When the applicant receives his written test results, a "Written Test Subject Matter Outline" will be included (see Table 1-1). This outline lists the codes and the meaning of each. For instance, the code B41 would mean the deficiency is in the area of weight and balance. From these codes, the applicant can determine the areas in which he needs review. In the event of failure, a flight instructor finds these codes invaluable in rebriefing the student for retesting.

It should be mentioned, as on all FAA tests, a 70 grade or better is passing. Everyone likes to make an "A" on tests, but, generally speaking, the results on the instrument exams run lower than any written exam administered by the FAA with the exception of the Airline Transport Pilot Written Exam. A grade of 70, however, is considered by almost everyone in the aviation training community to be as good as a grade of 90 or higher. What it boils down to is, everyone has a 30-point margin to pass the test and basically all that matters is whether you pass or fail. That's why I tell all of my students on a grade of 81, for example, that he's an 11-point genius. In general, FAA designee examiners or FAA inspectors are not impressed by high grades, though they may compliment you on good results. When it comes time for the flight check, your flight instructor will have gone over your deficiencies on the written test in order to have you adequately prepared for the oral test, and your deficiencies will have been eliminated.

WHERE DO THE EXAM QUESTIONS COME FROM?

If you have ever taken an FAA written examination or studied from any of the good aids available, you have probably asked yourself, "What's this question got to do with real flying?" In fact, in many cases the answer to that question is, "Not very much!" A little background is in order at this point. This could become very valuable in obtaining a passing score.

The FAA, like all government branches, prefers to delegate responsibility wherever and whenever possible in the name of job creation. The FAA has hired a staff of people with backgrounds in psychological testing to formulate their written exams. If these people have pilot backgrounds, that is merely coincidental to their position. In other words, the FAA Instrument Written Exam is drawn up and updated by persons that are professional test writers rather than professional pilots. Armed with this information, certain types of test questions can be attacked and better understood. It will be easier to arrive at the *most* correct choice instead of *just* a correct choice. In other words, attack the test as professional test-taker more so than a pilot.

The test questions themselves are generated from many sources. These sources are available to everyone for study, and knowing where to look is half the battle.

RECOMMENDED STUDY MATERIALS

Applicants for the Instrument Rating will find many good commercial publications and study aids. In fact, most people that will read this book may in fact be enrolled in an instrument ground school course. A formal ground school is the best way to obtain the information for the test

When preparing for the Instrument Rating, there are some sources that are invaluable. The foremost of these wells of information is the "Airman's Information Manual" (AIM). The manual is divided into five parts and presents information that is pertinent to preflight, departure, enroute, and arrival portions of all flights, IFR, as well as Visual Flight Regulations (VFR).

PART I—BASIC FLIGHT MANUAL AND ATC PROCEDURES

This manual is issued semiannually (January and July), so make sure you study a current issue because things to change. As a flight instructor, I put the heaviest emphasis on Part I. This portion of the AIM deals with the National Airspace System and the basic fundamentals of flight within the system. In addition, factors involving the safety of flight such as medical facts. All of the above mentioned information is important to passing the written exam but none is as important as the ATC information on IFR regulations and procedures. The ATC information is divided into preflight, departure, enroute, and arrival operations.

PART II—AIRPORT DIRECTORY

This part of the AIM is also issued semiannually (March and September). Make sure if you use this one for actual flight planning it is a current issue. Part II is an airport directory listing all airports, heliports, and floatplane bases available for civil use. The information is in coded form and one needs to understand the code in order to answer certain questions on the exam. A legend is portrayed in the front of the publication and really is easy to comprehend. Among the information presented in Part II is U.S. Entry and Departure Procedures listing Airports of Entry, telephone numbers of Flight Service Stations, and National Weather Service offices.

PART III—OPERATIONAL DATA

Part III, basically, is an airport facility directory of all major airports with control towers and instrument landing systems. Included in this part is a tabulation of Air Navigation Radio Aids and their restrictions, as well as a running list of new and permanently closed airports. Of the most valuable information to the pilot going IFR are the locations of VOR receiver check points, preferred IFR routes, and area navigation routes. Although there are questions on the Instrument Written Exam from this portion of the AIM, the usual "Question Selection Sheet" only includes one or two. Part III is issued every 56 days and will be extremely handy when planning an IFR flight, whether actual or for test application.

Part IIIA—NOTICES TO AIRMEN

Current "Notams" are essential to flight safety. Notices such as VORs out-of-service or runways closed for resurfacing are the bulk of this booklet. Part IIIA updates these notices every 14 days. As a result of the frequent updating, other data supplemental to the other four parts of the AIM are also included.

PART IV—GRAPHIC NOTICES AND SUPPLEMENTAL DATA

This part of the AIM contains information that remains fairly constant and is infrequently changed. It is updated quarterly beginning in January of each year. The information that may be gleaned from Part IV is a list of parachute jump areas, area graphics of airports having VFR arrival corridors such as Terminal Radar

Service Areas and graphic depictions of Terminal Control Areas.

The AIM is one of the most important sources of flight information on a daily basis, if not the most important. Up until recently, however, the cost of an annual subscription to all five parts has been a little steep for most weekend-type pilots. The annual rate has been about $32 per year. The FAA, realizing that use and subscription circulation of the AIM was decreasing, has taken it upon itself to alleviate the problem and ease a pilot's burden. Heretofore, the AIM has been published by the Government Printing Office and ordered through the Superintendent of Documents in Washington, D.C. Now, at the time of this writing, the FAA is taking over the printing and dissemination of Parts II and III of the AIM. The cost to pilots will be about $8 or $9 annually, a price that we can live with. The FAA hopes that this will put the AIM into more hands and increase its usage.

If you don't have your own subscription to the AIM, most FBOs do. I highly recommend that you sit down with a copy and become totally familiar with it before taking the written exam.

FEDERAL AVIATION REGULATIONS (FARS)

Ah yes, the FARs! What would a written exam be without the good old FARs? Though many parts exist, the FAA draws on three for testing purposes. Part 1 is Definitions and Abbreviations used in everyday aviation terminology. Part 61, lays out the ground rules for Airman Certification such as prerequisites and aeronautical knowledge required. Part 91, most drawn on by the FAA for testing, is entitled General Operating and Flight Rules and is just that. Of course, all questions will be geared to Instrument Flight Rules. Later in the book we'll deal with these rules of both Part 61 and 91, and the best way to remember items and keep them in line.

HANDBOOKS

There are many handbooks published by the FAA to aid the instrument student. Three of them are high recommended, and foremost is the *Instrument Flying Handbook*. This handbook is written with the reader in mind that holds at least a Private Pilot certificate. It covers all areas necessary to fully acquaint the student with information to become an instrument pilot. This particular publication has been a primary source for test questions for years.

Two handbooks that deal with weather are *Aviation Weather* and *Aviation Weather Services*. The former describes weather theory and meteorology as it applies to flying. The latter explains weather services available to pilots and the how's of interpreting and using reports such as hourly sequences, terminal forecasts, prognostic charts, and radar summaries. A great many questions on the Instrument Written Exam deal with the application of weather flying since instrument flying is weather flying. Because the FAA puts such great emphasis on this area on the test, we will discuss thoroughly how to best approach these questions.

CHARTS

Other information that is extremely pertinent to the written exam is the use and interpretation of navigation charts. The charts that appear on the exam are of the type published by the National Ocean Survey. Though the largest portion of the instrument pilot population uses Jeppesen-type charts, the government sticks with its own. If you haven't already begun flight training for instruments, it is best to learn the symbols for the NOS-type first. This will create less confusion in passing the written exam. It is my opinion that the written exam be taken early in flight training in order for the student to reap the greatest amount of knowledge from the instrument flight training itself.

If, however, you have already begun the flight portion of your instrument course, the transition to understanding NOS charts will be simplified if you realize that many of the symbols look much alike, but differ in that they are shaded in a manner opposite to one another. (See Fig. 1-1.)

The type charts one needs to familiarize himself with are the Enroute, Terminal, Approach, Standard Instrument Departures (SIDs), Standard Terminal Arrival Routes (STARs), and Low-Altitude Area Charts. Each one will be discussed later as they relate to specific questions on the written exam.

Some other information sources for questions as well as study aids are advisory circulars, Exam-O-Grams, and a source much used in composing this text, the Instrument Rating Written Test Guide (AC 61-8D). A list of the most applicable Advisory Circulars is included:

AC 00-2	Advisory Circular Checklist
AC 00-24	Thunderstorms
AC 61-84	Role of Preflight Preparation

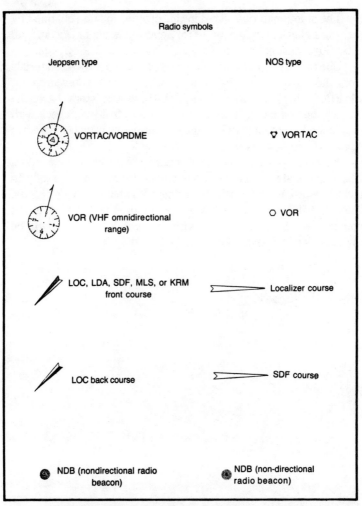

Fig. 1-1. A small example of how NOS charts compare with Jeppesen charts.

AC 90-12B	Severe Weather Avoidance
AC 90-14A	Altitude—Temperature Effect On Aircraft Performance
AC 90-62	Flying DME Arcs
AC 91-8A	Use of Oxygen by General Aviation Pilots/Passengers
AC 91.83-1A	Canceling or Closing Flight Plans

The study materials listed in this chapter may be obtained by sending a check or money order to: Superintendent of Documents, U.S. Government Printing Office, Washington, D.C. 20402.

Due to the length of time involved in receiving these materials from the Superintendent of Documents, I advise you search out all FBO's in your area. Many of these operators have the publications on hand. If your search proves fruitless, check with the General Aviation District Office because they usually have extra advisory circulars about, but no handbooks.

Now that you have been enlightened on what the test is and where the material for questions comes from, you are ready to tackle the task of making the Instrument Written Exam a bit easier. The task will not be simple, but with some sure-fire, tested methods, you can go into the test room with the confidence that it will be the only trip into that room you'll have to make.

Chapter 2

Weight and Balance

Weight and balance questions are frequently the most difficult in any FAA written exam. The FAA includes weight and balance problems in all tests from Private Pilot to Flight Engineer for large jets. Most weight and balance problems can be managed by a few basic formulas and just a few variations on those formulas.

Why weight and balance on an instrument written test? Well, IFR flight frequently takes more fuel than the same VFR flight. This is due to fuel required for alternate airports. Therefore, the useful load of an aircraft becomes restricted, and a pilot should be aware of this fact. Also, the test questions on the instrument written require more finesse than those on the Private Pilot exam. So, the FAA wants to see more knowledge and proficiency in their instrument certified pilots.

As you can well see, weight and balance are actually two terms. Weight—and—balance. When approaching these questions on the exam, it is best to separate them. First, solve for weight. Then solve for balance. This simplistic method will enable you to concentrate on only one set of number manipulations at a time and greatly reduce your chance for error.

In learning the methods to attack weight and balance, I will assume you have already achieved the status of Private Pilot and thus are familiar with basic weight and balance terms. First, let's look at weight. When I talk about weight, I am taking into consideration three terms:

- **Aircraft empty weight**. This is computed or actual weight provided by the manufacturer or a licensed mechanic who has weighed the plane. Usually this weight assumes all installed radio gear, unusable fuel, and undrainable oil.
- **Useful load**. This is the amount of fuel, crew, passengers, and baggage that can be added to the plane.
- **Gross weight**. This is the total weight of the aircraft at any given time, or a more precise term, "maximum allowable gross weight." Maximum allowable gross weight is the weight that is the loading weight limit of the aircraft.

Each pilot has access to the empty weight and maximum allowable gross weight of the airplane he is flying. This is the law. So it is no wonder that the information will be supplied on the test if it is needed.

WEIGHT AND BALANCE BY COMPUTATION

Now, let's look at a simple weight problem. Given the following date is the airplane within its maximum allowable gross weight of 2,800 lbs?

Empty weight	1900 lbs.
Pilot and front passenger	340 lbs.
Rear passenger(s)	250 lbs.
Fuel (38 gals.)	
Oil (8 qts.)	
Baggage	37 lbs.
Total	

This is a very simple problem similar to those on the Private Pilot Written Exam. It has everything included that one needs to work with, except the fuel and oil conversion factors. These conversions must be committed to memory by rote. Fuel weighs 6 lbs. per gallon. Oil weighs 7.5 lbs. per gallon. Once all factors are known and have been computed, the problem is simple addition resulting in a total gross weight. The way to approach this problem is to formulate a plan of attack that won't let you down.

A method I learned while in attendance at a Bill Phelps Airline Ground School for Flight Engineer works very well, even on simple problems. It goes like this:

1) **See the target clearly!** You must read the question carefully and decide what the question specifically asks. In our example the question is; "Is the airplane within allowable gross weight limits?" The only way you'll know the target is to *read the friggin' question* (RTFQ)! So, remember, on each question RTFQ is rule number one.

2) **Plan a checklist.** As pilots, we are used to flying with a checklist. Why not use one when taking a test on flying. This means you need to list the things needed to answer the target question. In this case you need to know a) empty weight, b) maximum allowable gross weight, c) weight of all passengers plus the pilot, d) weight of all fuel and oil, e) baggage weight if any. The idea here is if you can answer each item on the checklist you can arrive at the target.

In the version of the FAA test currently in use, the FAA has made the task of coming up with the checklist very easy. The checklist is made up for you on the charts that supply information. They are labeled B-3, B-4, etc. Anywhere a blank exists on these checklists, you can assume that no weight occupies that datum position.

a) **Is it given?** Now that a checklist has been established, ask the above question on each count, such as empty weight (is it given?). Yes, is the answer. I'm not suggesting that you write each part of the checklist out, because it is already before you on the test. Here's how it could be pictured in your mind:

Checklist	Is it given?	
Maximum allowable gr. wt.	(Yes)	No
Empty weight	(Yes)	No
Weight of passengers & pilot	(Yes)	No
Weight of fuel	Yes	(No)
Weight of oil	Yes	(No)
Weight of baggage	(Yes)	No

From doing this, you can now plainly identify which items need further attention and are in your way of reaching the target.

b) **Directly from knowing?** Having identified the parts of the problem needing further attention, you must ask the next question. Weight of the fuel was not given as shown on my checklist. If it is not given, you must compute it. The weight of fuel can be computed *directly from knowing—* weight of fuel in pounds per gallon or 6 lbs. per gallon as discussed earlier. Now, plug in the numbers. Thirty-eight gallons times 6 lbs. equals 228 lbs.

The weight of oil was not given. Can you ascertain that weight *directly from knowing*? Of course you can! Oil weighs 7.5 lbs. per gallon. This is where it gets involved and tricky. The test question didn't give you gallons of oil. It gave you quarts! What now? Follow the plan of attack. How many gallons? (Is it given?) Yes (No). You know 8 quarts to be given. Can you find the number of gallons *directly from knowing* the number of quarts. Sure, there are 4 quarts to the gallon. Eight divided by 4 equals 2 gallons.

From here all you do is plug in the numbers. Multiply 7.5 times 2 gallons. The answer is 15 lbs.

Now! *All* of the questions have been answered except the target. Now sum all of your weights and arrive at the total of 2,770 lbs. The target question was "Is the airplane within allowable gross weight limits?" The answer is Yes, the airplane is within allowable gross weight limits, because 2,770 lbs. is less than 2,800 lbs.

I'm sure all of that seemed rather involved for a simple gross weight problem. If you missed some of it, go back and read it over until you understand it. Basically, the rest of this chapter will deal with using this principal. Bill Phelps has achieved extremely high rates of passing by using this method. It *will* work for you. Now, without all of that other garbage around the main words, let's examine the plan of attack unobstructed. Everyone has a photographic memory whether you can use it or not. If you look at this simple method printed out, you will remember it.

R.T.F.Q.

1) **See the target clearly!**
2) **Plan a checklist.**
   a) **Is it given?**
   b) **Directly from knowing?**

If the answer to Part b is no or incomplete, return to Part a, etc.

Next, I will discuss balance. Balance is not independent of weight. It is tied to weight by the formula: weight times arm = Moment.

$$(\text{wt.} \times \text{arm} = M)$$

In computing the balance point of anything, whether it be a steel beam, a car, and in this book, airplanes, several mathematic functions must be performed. The purpose of this discussion is to show you an easy method for remembering first the formula, then performing the mathematics in proper order to arrive at the *center of gravity* (CG). But first, let's review what CG is and how it is measured.

In airplanes (and on the test), all stations of loading weight are measured from a common starting point called the *datum plane*. A loading station, for example, would be a rear seat passenger or forward baggage compartment. So, a rear seat passenger is so many inches from the datum. The datum plane is arbitrarily chosen by the manufacturer's engineers. In light, general aviation aircraft, the datum is usually at the tip of the prop spinner or at the engine firewall. The FAA tests seem to prefer the latter. After the aircraft is loaded with passengers, fuel, and baggage, the center of gravity will fall at some point.

To make this simple, you could consider an aircraft to be just a wooden beam (see Fig. 2-1). The left end as you face the beam will be the datum. If you hung a small weight from the beam, say, on the right side, the beam would tip to the right. If you were to balance this beam, you would have to shift the point of balance (CG) to the right towards the weight and away from the datum. And so it goes. As a new weight would be added, the CG would consistently move towards that weight some unknown distance (see Fig. 2-1).

To find what that unknown distance would be, you have to use the formula mentioned earlier. Weight × arm = Moment. Weight is calculated from addition, as done earlier in the chapter. *Arm* is the measurable distance a weight is stationed from the datum. It can be a positive distance or a negative distance depending on the side it is placed from the datum. When solving for CG, you solve for the arm. *Moments* are a little harder to understand. Simply put, moments are the force that tends to turn an unbalanced beam about some unknown point. For instance, when you tighten a nut with a wrench, the force you put on the handle of the wrench to turn the nut is the moment (see Fig. 2-2). Another example; if you had a wooden beam balanced on your finger and added a weight to the right side, the right end would start to turn around your finger.

Moments sometimes become very large numbers. For example, 340 lbs. at station 64 (64 inches from datum) equals a moment of 21,760 in-lbs. Due to the difficulty of working with numbers of this size you will often see the *moment index* (MOM/1000). A moment

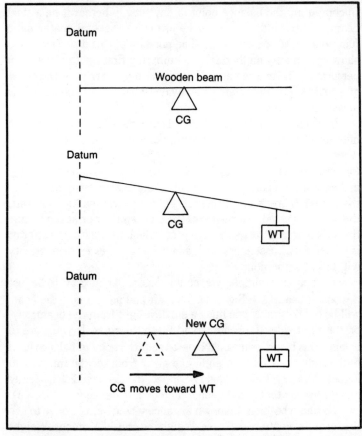

Fig. 2-1. When weight is added to the beam, the center of gravity moves towards that weight as shown in the bottom figure.

index is nothing more than dividing the moment by 1,000 to make it more manageable or smaller, if you will. Thus, 21,760 in-lbs. will be represented as 21.76 MOM/1000.

To remember the balance formula, I'd like to take you back a few years. Think about your grandmother. What a dear, sweet lady. Can you remember how you used to write her when you were a kid? Back when long distance telephone calls weren't cheap? How did you sign your letters to her? I bet you used love and kisses, right? Remember the little xxxx's that stood for kisses. That's our memory aid; those little xxxx's.

Here's how you will use them to remember my formula and order of operations:

$$\text{Weight will kiss your} \quad \text{a great moment}$$
$$\text{Wt.} \times \text{arm} = \overline{\text{M}}$$

Simply read; weight will kiss your arm and equal a great moment. Silly, isn't it? Just silly enough that if you will now repeat it twice to yourself, out loud, I guarantee you will always remember it. Don't forget to check around the corner so that nobody sees you practicing. Again, this is a technique I learned from Floyd at Airline Ground Schools. It worked well enough to get me a grade of 98 on the Flight Engineer Exam. It will work for you!

This is the way you remember the formula for finding the center of gravity. The thing to do from here is build upon our aid until you have covered all mathematical operations. So, let's do it again adding some things to it step by step.

$$\text{kiss your} \quad \text{great}$$
$$\text{Wt.} \times \text{arm} = \overline{\text{M}}$$
$$| \quad\quad\quad\quad |$$

The lines indicate two columns of numbers. To make this work, you should draw this out on scratch paper. For practice, and for

Fig. 2-2. The Moment works through the end of the wrench and causes a turning motion.

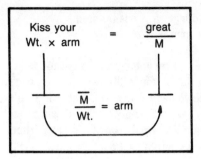

Fig. 2-3. Stick the weights into the moments.

real in the test room, say, "two columns of numbers."

Next, you must *underscore the outboards*.

$$\underline{\text{kiss your}} \quad \underline{\text{great}}$$
$$\text{Wt.} \times \text{arm} \quad = \quad \overline{\text{M}}$$

Once again, to incorporate this into your photographic memory, say, "underscore the outboards."

Bringing sex into play, you will also be able to aid your memory. Say, "stick the weights into the moments." (See Fig. 2-3).

That concludes learning the operation. Once you "stick the weights into the moments," (meaning divide) the result you are left with is the arm or center of gravity.

In a nutshell, write the formula down then add "two columns of numbers" and stick the total weights into the total moments. After division, your answer is the CG for the aircraft.

Let's try a problem now and see how our memory aid works. Here's a problem right from the FAA Instrument Written Exam.

What is the CG in inches aft of datum for operating conditions B-1? (use Table 2-1 and Fig. 2-4).

1. 33.91"
2. 34.68"
3. 35.38"
4. 36.01"

In answering this problem you must refer to the correct chart, supplied in this case as B-1 on (Table 2-1). Approaching this problem is easy if you use the checklist procedure—R.T.F.Q. first!

1) **See the Target Clearly!** Obviously, you need to solve for

18

Table 2-1. Weight and Balance Data.

WEIGHT & BALANCE

OPERATING CONDITIONS			B-1	B-2	B-3	B-4	B-5	B-6
Seats	1 2	Arm = 37"	170 160	180 130	165 150	150 165	175 170	200 180
Seats	3 4	Arm = 68"		50 30	170 180	180 200		120
Seats	3 4	Arm = 71"						
Seats	5 6	Arm = 102"		40 30				
Baggage	Nose Compartment	Arm – 96"	110	50	50	40		30
	Wing Locker	Arm – 124"		30	60	10	60	
		Arm – 126"			30	50		50
Fuel	Main Wing Tanks		100	100	100	100	85	100
	Aux. Wing Tanks		63	63	63	50	50	60
	Wing Locker Tanks		–	40	20	–	–	20

NOTE: All operating conditions are stated in pounds except fuel, which is given in gallons.

19

CG in inches aft of datum. There are no hidden factors to consider here.

2) Plan a Checklist.
a) Is it Given?
b) Directly from Knowing?

In this new format, the FAA has simplified things a great deal. Be careful when copying numbers from any of the charts,however, especially those from Fig. 2-4.

Here's how the checklist should look with this problem:

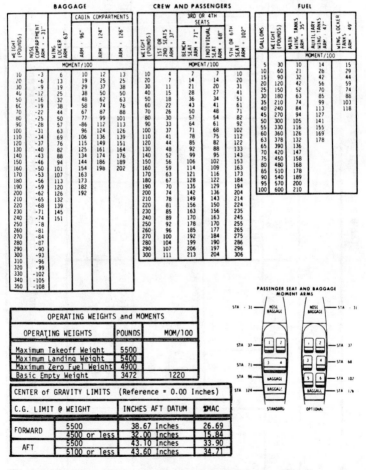

Fig. 2-4. Weight and Moment table showing positoins on aircraft.

	kiss your	great
	WT. × ARM =	$\overline{M}$
Empty weight	Given	Given
*Oil	Given	Given
Fuel	Given in gals.	Given or directly from knowing
Pilot & Copilot	Given	Given
Passengers	Given	Given
Baggage	Given	Given

*Oil—weight and MOM included in aircraft basic empty weight. The key to knowing this is the term *basic*. Whenever you see that term, certain basic things are included in the empty weight. Because oil is not listed anywhere on any chart, then oil is included in the basic empty weight.

Checking over the checklist, I find that everything is given on the charts. Therefore, all you need to do is sum the weights and the moments in each column by "underscoring the outboards."

		kiss your	great
		WT. × ARM =	$\overline{M}$
Basic Empty Weight		3,472 =	1220
Fuel	main	600 × 35 =	210
	aux	378 × 47 =	178
Pilot & Copilot		330 × 37 =	122
Passengers		0 × 0 =	0
Baggage		110 × −31 =	− 34
		4,890	1,696

After the columns have been totaled, you must stick the weights into the moments to arrive at the center of gravity. Also, note that the negative moments must be subtracted from the various positive moments. At this time, it is also necessary to add two zeroes to the moments so that computation looks like this:

$$\frac{169,600}{4,890} = \frac{34.68''}{\text{C.G.}}$$

Now, compare your answer with the list of answers following

the question to find out if you have worked or solved the problem correctly. You will find that choice No. 2 is the correct answer.

For practice, try these next questions using the procedure above as a model. Refer to Table 2-1 and Fig. 2-4.

What is the CG in inches aft of datum for operating conditions B-2?

1. 37.03″
2. 37.67″
3. 38.00″
4. 38.99″

The proper choice for this question is No. 2. Your final division should look like this:

$$\frac{19700}{5230} = 37.66''$$

What is the CG in inches aft of datum for operations conditions B-3?

1. 38.73″
2. 39.03″
3. 39.23″
4. 39.89″

Your final division should look like this:

$$\frac{207.600}{5375} = 38.62''$$

The correct choice is No. 1. The only choice that is close is 38.73″; all of the answers are in the 39″ range, and thus, the FAA wants the closest answer chosen to their computations.

WEIGHT AND BALANCE BY GRAPH

We have already learned to compute weight and balance by the conputation method. The FAA will provide you with ample opportunities to show your knowledge of weight and balance. The graph method is a quick way to find your CG, though it may not have the accuracy of the former method.

Having already given yourself over to the plan of attack, you can approach a graph loading problem in the same way as before. Here is a graph problem from the FAA Instrument Exam:

Calculate the total weight and moment and determine if it is within the limits of the CG Envelope (See Fig. 2-5).

Empty weight—2520 lbs., with moment 90.3/1000 in-lbs.
Oil—21 lbs at —0.3 moment

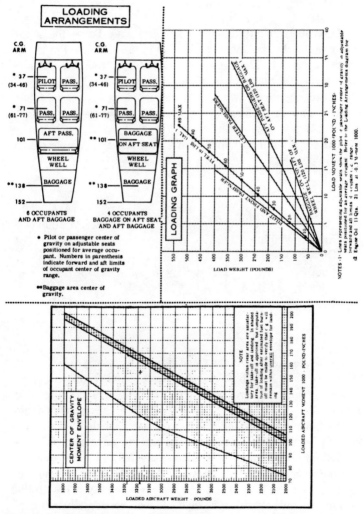

Fig. 2-5. An easy to calculate method for weight and balance employs graphs.

Fuel—89 gal. at 6 lbs./gal.
Pilot and front passenger—400 lbs.

	Weight	MOM/1000	Within Limits
1.	3433	137.5	Yes
2.	3475	127.5	Yes
3.	3433	128.1	No
4.	3475	127.5	No

As on all exam questions, begin by R.T.F.Q. To see the target clearly, just read the question because in this instance the target is quite apparent. The target—"Calculate the total weight and moment and determine if it is within the limits of the CG Envelope." The target mentions two things discussed earlier, weight and moment. Those two things are products of the weight and balance formula, Wt. × arm = $\overline{M}$

The second thing to do is plan a checklist and complete it as much as possible.

	kiss your		great
	Wt. × arm	=	$\overline{M}$
			MOM 1000
Empty Weight	2⎪250		90⎪.3
Oil	⎪021		−⎪.3
Fuel	89 gal. × 6 lbs.		22⎪.8
Pilot &			
Passenger	⎪400		14⎪.75
	3,475		127.55

Complete the checklist in the usual manner by asking a) Is it given? b) Directly from knowing? The fuel moment and the pilot and front passenger moment are not given. Directly from knowing is answered by going to the "Loading Graph." The moment index can be found by following the appropriately labeled line such as fuel or pilot and front passenger. The fuel line on this graph is also divided into the number of gallons. This makes it even easier to find the moment index. Because 89 gallons was given, you only have to go to the 89 gallon point and read directly below to find the moment index. Although you could read horizontally to the left and find the fuel weight, there could be some error. The best way to find the fuel weight would be to multiply 89 gals. × 6 lbs. per gal. = 534 lbs. This eliminates chart reading error. After doing that operation, "underscore the outboards" and sum your weights and moments. In a graph problem, the similarity to the computation method stops here. You don't "stick the weights into the moments." Instead, you go to the graph labeled "Center of Gravity Moment Envelope."

The "Center of Gravity Moment Envelope" is a graph of loaded aircraft weight plotted against the loaded aircraft moments. The moments lie along the bottom of the graph, while the weights are vertically displayed along the left side of the graph. Having summed the weights and moments, take one or the other and go to the graph. This method you probably learned as a private pilot, but I will review it. First, take the 3,475 lbs. and enter the graph from the left until you meet the 127.5 moment index entered from the bottom. If the two lines intersect inside the heavy lines, the aircraft is within center of gravity limits. If they intersect outside the heavy lines of the envelope, the aircraft is out of center of gravity limits. In the 200 sample problem, the lines intersect outside the envelope, meaning the aircraft is not in limits.

Going to the list of possible answers, you will find two answers that have your calculated gross weight and your sum of moments. They are answer Nos. 2 and 4. Answer No. 2 says the aircraft is in limits and No. 4 says it is out of limits. Therefore, you must choose answer No. 4. Once again, the FAA is ready to take advantage of your haste. If you would have just glanced at the answers after computing your weights and moments, an incorrect choice could have been made. See the problem all of the way through, and you'll do fine. Don't hurry!

WEIGHT SHIFT PROBLEMS

Up to this point, the weight and balance problems have been of the same type that are on the Private Pilot Written Exam. As explained earlier though, the FAA expects a higher level of performance and demonstrated knowledge from its instrument rated pilots. That is why they include weight shift problems in the written exam.

The basic weight shift formula is:

$$\frac{\text{Weight to be shifted}}{\text{Total Gross Weight}} = \frac{\text{Distance CG changes } \Delta}{\text{Distance the weight shifted}}$$

The symbol Δ is called *delta* and stands for change. A somewhat simplified way to remember this formula would be:

$$\frac{\text{Little weight}}{\text{Big weight}} = \frac{\text{Distance CG } \Delta}{\text{Distance weight shifted}}$$

Either of these forms of the formula must be memorized to take into the test room. Now, let's attempt a weight shift problem, one that comes from the written exam, of course.

This airplane is ready for an IFR flight with these conditions:

Loaded weight—2,650 lbs.
Loaded center of gravity—62.7" aft of datum.

Before departure, these changes to loading are made:

30 gallons of aviation gas added to tanks at 67.5" aft of datum.
40 lbs of baggage removed from a compartment 147.2" aft of datum.

What is the new center of gravity?

1. 67.0" aft of datum
2. 65.2" aft of datum
3. 63.1" aft of datum
4. 61.8" aft of datum

Back to basics again.

1) **See the target clearly!** What is the new CG?
2) **Plan a checklist.**

$$\frac{\text{Weight to be shifted}}{\text{Total Gross Weight}} = \frac{\text{Distance CG } \Delta}{\text{Distance weight shifted}}$$

a) **Is it given?**
b) **Directly from knowing?**

By going directly to my formula and using it is your checklist, let's ask questions:

1) **The weight to be shifted—Is it given?** Yes, but not in a way the formula can digest it. First off, you have two different

weights that are changing, the 30-gallons of fuel and the 40 lbs. of baggage, one of which you will have to solve like this: 30 gals. × 6 lbs. per gal. = 180 lbs. The two different weights indicate you will have to do two complete and separate operations of the formula. Double jeopardy so to speak.

2) **Total Gross Weight—Is it given?** It sure is—2,650 lbs. That was easy.

3) **Distance CG changed—Is it given?** No, this is not given. Can you find it directly from knowing anything? Sure, you can. If you know the weight shift formula and have all of the other blanks filled in, you can simply solve for the unknown part of the formula.

4) **Distance weight shifted—Is it given?** Not exactly. You need to know some basic balance techniques. Remember early in the chapter when I discussed balancing a beam on your finger? I said that the CG will move toward the weight added; thus, the 180 lbs. of fuel will be added at 67.5″ aft of datum and the CG will move from 62.7″ aft of datum towards 67.5″ aft of datum some unknown distance. The baggage at 147.2″ aft of datum is no longer on the plane after the fuel has been added and, therefore, has no moment at all. Thus, the net weight shift from removing the baggage will be towards the datum, a negative direction. You must consider this later on.

Plugging in the numbers for the first operation of adding fuel looks like this:

$$\frac{180 \text{ lbs.}}{2650 \text{ lbs.}} = \frac{\text{Distance CG}\Delta}{67.5''}$$
$$4.6'' = \text{Distance CG changed}$$

Now, you must consider the baggage being removed. The numbers must change, especially the Total Gross Weight. Remember, the fuel was added, making the total weight 2830 lbs.

$$\frac{40 \text{ lbs.}}{2830 \text{ lbs.}} = \frac{\text{Distance CG }\Delta''}{147.2''}$$
$$-2.08 = \text{Distance CG }\Delta''$$

The value above is negative because the weight was removed from 147.2″ and went to 0″ at the datum. A move in a negative direction.

The new CG is equal to the old CG plus the net change. Like this:

$$\underset{62.7''}{\text{Old CG}} + \underset{(4.6'' - 2.08'')}{\text{Net Change}} = \text{New CG}$$

$$65.22'' \text{ aft of datum} = \text{New CG}$$

Going to the list of answers you will find 65.2″ aft of datum, answer No. 2, to be the closest to your 65.22″ aft of datum. You should choose No 2 to the low side not only because it is close, but also because the FAA would consider an aircraft close to its aft CG limit to be the most unstable in flight, requiring close scrutiny by the pilot in command. Remember that all numerical problems of the exam are worked according to three different types of computers. It could be the answer they chose was done with a different type of instrument.

Some weight shift problems are easier to approach and less involved than the previous one. Here's my final example of weight shift:

Your airplane is loaded to gross weight of 5,000 lbs., with three pieces of luggage in the rear baggage compartment. You determine the CG is 98″ aft of datum, which is 2″ aft of limits. If you move two pieces of luggage, which together weigh 100 lbs., from the rear baggage compartment (145″ aft of datum) to the front compartment (45″aft of datum) what is the new CG?

1. 95.8″ aft of datum
2. 96.0″ aft of datum
3. 96.5″ aft of datum
4. 97.0″ aft of datum

Again, begin with the plan of attack.

1) **See the target clearly!** What is the new CG?
2) **Plan a checklist.**

$$\frac{\text{Weight to be shifted}}{\text{Total Gross Weight}} = \frac{\text{Distance CG changed}}{\text{Distance weight shifted}}$$

a) **Is it given?**
b) **Directly from knowing?**

In this problem:

1) **Weight to be shifted—Is it given?** Yes, 100 lbs. of baggage is to be moved.
2) **Total Gross Weight—Is it given?** Yes, 5,000 lbs. total gross weight.
3) **Distance CG changed—Is it given?** No. Can you find it directly from knowing? Yes, if you know the other three portions of the formula you can solve for it.
4) **Distance weight shifted—Is it given?** No. Can you find it directly from knowing? Yes, you know where it was originally placed, as well as where it ended up. It moved from 145″ aft of datum to 45″ aft of datum. The move was toward the datum thus note that the CG change will also be in that direction.

Plug in the numbers and it looks like this:

$$\frac{100 \text{ lbs.}}{5000 \text{ lbs.}} = \frac{\text{Distance CG changed}}{(145″ - 45″)}$$

$$2″ = \text{Distance CG changed}$$

$$\begin{aligned} \text{New CG} &= \text{Old CG} - \text{net change} \\ &= 98″ - 2″ \\ &= 96″ \text{ aft of datum} \end{aligned}$$

The answer choices indicate answer No. 2 is correct.

You have now examined the full gamut of the FAA bag of tricks on weight and balance. The problems are not difficult when following the "plan of attack," because it leads you through each problem in a logical manner. I didn't invent this "plan of attack," but I wish I had. I implore you to follow it as it has been laid out. It has worked so well for so many others that I'm sure it will work for you.

At this point, I advise you to obtain a copy of the Instrument Rating Written Test Guide (AC 61-8D), and work the other problems supplied therein. The time and effort will be reflected in your test results, and remember, the idea of this book is for you to only have to take the test once.

Chapter 3

Remembering the FARS

There are not too many gimmicks for remembering the Federal Aviation Regulations, although there are some. As I discuss these rules and regulations, I will also discuss the best way to remember them where applicable. Most rules have been devised from common sense and errors that were made in actual flight situations. After examining the FARs, as an instructor, it has become apparent to me that the rules are fairly lenient. In a society such as ours, the government, at least in this case, has endeavored to control us as little as possible while supplying us with much needed guidelines for safety. Though many in the pilot population cry "over-restriction," the few absolute restrictions that there are on the airways are needed. They are needed to protect us from ourselves as well as the other guy. Prudent aircraft operation in the future will certainly reduce the amount of legislation forced upon us.

Let's take a look at those FAA bugaboos, the FARs. The Federal Aviation Regulations are divided into many parts. The FAA will test you on two of those parts. Part 61 is the book of rules concerning airman certification. When you trained for your Private Pilot license there were certain requirements that had to be met, such as the amount of nighttime flight you needed, or how much solo cross-country. These rules, though rarely thought about except when training for a new rating, constitute the foundation for the kind of pilot that you are. The knowledge that a pilot applicant must display on a written exam and the oral exam before the flight test, is prescribed in Part 61. Generally, if the pilot has the aeronautical knowledge prescribed in Part 61 and retains it, the safer, more professional pilot he remains. Also, knowing Part 61 for the rating you are training for will help save you money. If a pilot knows ahead of time what the requirements are for the rating he desires, over-instruction can be avoided.

Part 91, is called "General Operating and Flight Rules." Part 91, in fact, is much of the material Part 61 prescribes. In relation to the IFR rating, Part 91, focuses on points such as IFR flight, fuel required for certain operations, or landing and takeoff minima. What it comes right down to is, Part 91 is the guts of the Instrument Rating. In fact, so many times throughout the Instrument Written Exam, the question that one is working on may not be answered correctly unless he has a full working knowledge of Part 91. For instance, a problem of weight and balance mentions the fuel to destination as well as the alternate. If the student forgot to also add the mandatory 45- minute reserve after reaching the alternate, he or she would invariably compute an incorrect answer.

So, that is what Part 61 and Part 91 is in a nutshell. Sometimes they are a source of confusion, and sometimes a refreshing drink in the heat of an informationless desert.

PART 61

What does Part 61 say about becoming IFR-rated in plain English? I will discuss it now in everyday terms. Hopefully, discussing it this way, you will remember some of it for the test. Part 61.65 lays out the requirements for the instrument rating. Don't worry about the number; you will never need to know it.

To be eligible for the instrument rating, one must hold either a Private Pilot or Commercial Pilot license, in the category of aircraft such as helicopter or airplane, according to the rating sought. You must be able to read, speak, and understand the English language. (I know some good ol' boys down in southern Louisiana, and I'm not sure that what they are speaking is English, but they fly pretty good.)

Assuming one meets the above requirements, he must have logged some ground instruction. This may be either from an approved school or a home study course. The knowledge one must have retained must be in the area of Federal Aviation Regulations that apply to IFR flight. You must have knowledge of the Airman's Information Manual and the IFR air traffic system and procedures.

Also, in order to pass the written exam, each applicant needs to know dead reckoning as it would apply to IFR navigation, navigation by VOR, ADF, and ILS systems, as well as the use of IFR charts and approach plates as they apply to those types of navigation.

Because instrument flying is weather flying it would seem appropriate to know something about the weather. I encourage everyone to learn as much as possible on the subject because it will allow you to live longer. On the other hand, the FAA says the minimum knowledge is the use of weather reports and forecasts and an elementary knowledge of forecasting weather trends on the basis of that information, as well as personal observation. Believe me, what you *see* out the window of your aircraft is far more important than what was forecast to be out the window two hours ago.

Unfortunately, the written examination will also include questions on the requirements necessary to take the flight check. An applicant for the flight test must present a logbook certified by a flight instructor showing he has received the necessary instruction in an airplane and has been found competent to take the flight test.

The area of skill in which one must show proficiency is the control and maneuvering of an airplane solely by instrument reference. That's not too much to ask. If you couldn't at least do that much the sky would be raining instrument (?) pilots. The idea of the national navigation system is to get from point A to point B. The system is made of various VORs and ADF systems. Therefore, the FAA expects you to be able to navigate using these facilities, including compliance with ATC instructions and procedures.

Once you get to point B, you need to get down out of the clouds. There are three types of approaches, basically. These are the VOR, ADF or NDB, and the ILS. The inspector will expect you to shoot the approaches down to published minimums.

The instrument cross-country is an important aspect of the instrument training regimen. It will come late in the instrument trainee's program. The purpose of it is to give the instructor a look at how the student performs in the real world of flying place to place. A student will have to deal with obtaining clearances, enroute procedures, and arrival procedures. It calls for the student to be prepared for all eventualities of the instrument environment. Additionally, it is a requirement for which you, the student, must show record for at the time of your flight examination. This cross-country flight must be 250 miles long and two of the airports must be 100 miles from each other. The flight can be made in either simulated or actual instrument conditions on Federal Airways or as routed by ATC. There must be one approach shot at each airport consisting of VOR, ADF, or ILS. When the trip is completed, all three types of approaches will have been done.

Be sure you have filled this requirement before your instrument flight check. Believe me, the examiner *will* send you back out to do it. At the cost per hour of today's instruction and light planes, the shock of additional required training is not just an emotional one—it will be a financial one.

What would a flight check be without simulated emergencies? There will be some on the instrument rating flight check. These will include recovery from unusual altitudes, loss of communications, equipment and instrument malfunctions, missed approach procedures, and engine-out emergencies if you use a multi-engine aircraft.

That covers all of the areas of aeronautical knowledge you must possess. It doesn't sound like much, but it's the fine points that get you. Moving on through the rest of 61.65 you come to flight experience. Knowing this subject may also save you money by helping you side-step flight instruction you don't need.

The applicant for the instrument rating must have a total of at least 125 hours of flight time, including at least 50 hours of cross-country time during which the applicant was pilot in command. All cross-country flights must be at least 50 nautical miles long to count toward this requirement. The cross-country requirement of 50 hours must be in the same category of aircraft in which the rating is sought. Which means if the instrument rating is sought for an airplane, you must have 50 hours of cross-country in airplanes.

You will also need 40 hours of simulated or actual instrument time, of which not more than 20 hours may be instrument dual instruction on an approved ground trainer. Some of these table top instrument simulators are approved and will definitely save you money while making you a competent pilot, but, remember, only 20 hours can be counted towards the instrument rating. Referring back to the 40 hours of instrument time, note that all of that time is not required to be dual given by an instructor. That's another loophole to save you some of your hard earned bucks. Only 15 hours of instrument instruction by a certified instrument instructor is required. Five hours of that must be in airplanes. You can assume the other 10 hours of dual could be given to you on a simulator.

That completes the look at Part 61.65. Let's take a look at a couple of typical FAA questions out of the written exam. These questions generally attack the definition of instrument flight. This is important, so read it carefully and remember it. This may be the only place you ever see it.

Instrument Flight. Flight in weather conditions that are less than those prescribed for basic VFR flight. Also, conditions in which aircraft control must be maintained by reference to instruments solely.

The last sentence of the definition may be very important after you have obtained your IFR rating. It says, in essence, that you may log actual flight time whenever you maintain aircraft control solely by instrument reference. For example, a flight over a large body of water in hazy conditions where the horizon is not discernible is legal instrument flight and can be logged as such. You don't have to be in clouds to log actual instrument flight time.

But back to the definition. If you understand its implications, then it becomes easy to choose the correct choice on the exam. Here's a sample test question:

The pilot in command of a civil aircraft must have an instrument rating only when operating . . .

1. under instrument flight rules, in weather conditions less than the minimum prescribed for VFR flight, and in a positive control area or route segment.
2. in controlled airspace in weather conditions less than the minimum prescribed for VFR flight.
3. in controlled airspace when operating under instrument flight rules.
4. in weather conditions less than the minimum prescribed for VFR flight.

The correct choice in this question is No. 1. Answer No. 1 actually includes the other three possible answers as well as including a reservation for positive control area. The positive control area being referred to is the altitudes above FL 180, and all flights in that airspace must be on an instrument flight plan. Accordingly, you must be instrument rated to even file IFR.

Which flight operation, below 18,000 feet, requires the pilot in command to be instrument rated?

1. A flight operation in a control zone when passengers are carried in weather conditions less than basic VFR.
2. Any flight operation where the pilot in command controls the airplane solely by reference to flight instruments.
3. A flight operation in weather conditions less than the minimums prescribed for VFR flight or under instrument flight rules.
4. Any flight operation in controlled airspace where controlled by ATC.

Answer No. 3 is *most* correct. Choice No. 1 is correct except it doesn't matter whether you carry passengers or not. Remember, if conditions are less than VFR minimums, or if you *file* IFR, you must be instrument rated.

Another favorite target of the FAA is Part 61.57. This paragraph of the FARs refers to instrument recency of experience. It states; "within the last six months, a pilot may not act as pilot in command in instrument conditions unless he has logged six hours of instrument time under actual or simulated IFR conditions. In addition to that six hours, he must have logged at least six approaches or passed an instrument competency check."

Sorting through all of that, I come up with a memory technique to always get the question right. It is called the "triple six method." Simply stated a pilot needs:

> six hours and
> six approaches in
> six months

Only three approaches and half the flight time may be on an instrument simulator. If you think you've got that, let's try an actual sample question.

To meet the minimum required instrument experience to remain current for IFR operations, you must accomplish during the past six months at least . . .

1. six instrument approaches and six hours of instrument time in any aircraft.
2. six instrument approaches and six hours of instrument time; three hours of the instrument time must be in the category of aircraft to be flown.
3. six instrument approaches, three of which must be in the same

category and class of aircraft to be flown, and six hours of instrument time in any aircraft.

4. six instrument approaches, three of which must be in the same category of aircraft to be flown; and six hours of instrument time, three hours of which must be in the same category of aircraft to be flown.

Choice No. 4 is most correct because it includes six approaches, six hours, and the "one half flight time must be in the same aircraft category" rule.

Some other areas that the FAA is now testing are general knowledge areas of Part 61. For examples, answer the following questions.

To carry passengers for hire in airplane on cross-country flights of more than 50 nautical miles from the departure airport, the pilot in command is required to hold at least a Commercial Pilot Certificate and . . .

1. a Category A pilot authorization.
2. a Category II pilot authorization.
3. a First-Class Medical Certificate.
4. an instrument pilot rating.

The correct answer is No. 4. This answer is not so much a necessary part of the instrument curriculum, but is more appropriately a corollary of the commercial pilot certificate requirements. Nonetheless, the FAA in most recent times has chosen to become more hardline on all aviation matters. Thus, you are required to know 61.129 even though you may never attain commercial pilot status or desire to do so.

PART 91

As discussed earlier, Part 91 is a large part of the written exam. The FAA will not only ask questions directly testing your knowledge of the subject, but will also subtly expect you to know how Part 91 fits in with preflight action. In other words, when you fill in the flight log on the exam, you will need to know Part 91 to do it correctly.

The exam questions that are directed specifically at Part 91 are divided into three areas. Those areas are: preflight action for flight, preflight action for aircraft, and flight planning. A few of those questions will also deal with information in the Airman's Information Manual.

Paragraph 91.5 of the FARs is a broad and all encompassing rule. It simply states that the pilot must familiarize himself or herself with *all* available information concerning that flight. That information must include, for a flight under IFR, weather reports and forecasts, fuel requirements, and alternates available if the flight cannot be completed as you planned. In addition, the runway lengths at the destination airport must be known as well as whether or not your airplane is able to operate in and out of that airport safely. Don't forget known traffic delays. You must also plan for them.

Before beginning any flight under IFR, the pilot in command must become familiar with all available information concerning that flight. In addition, the pilot must . . .

1. list an alternate airport on the flight plan and become familiar with the instrument approaches to that airport.
2. list an alternate airport in the flight plan and confirm adequate takeoff and landing performance at the destination airport.
3. be familiar with all instrument approaches at the destination airport.
4. be familiar with the runway lengths at airports of intended use, and the alternatives available if the flight cannot be completed.

Choice No. 4 is correct. As in the paragraph above, it deals with 91.5.

One of the most difficult areas of understanding comes from 91.23. It is very easy to become confused. I will try to sort it out and keep it straight. Fundamentally, it says to fly IFR, considering weather reports and forecasts, as well as weather conditions, a pilot must carry enough fuel to . . .

- complete the flight to the first airport of intended landing (the destination),
- fly from the destination airport to the alternate airport, and
- fly thereafter for 45 minutes at normal cruising speed.

The necessary fuel required to fly to the alternate is not required, however, if the following conditions exist: the forecast at the first airport of intended landing from one hour before to one hour after must call for the ceiling to be at least 2,000 feet above airport elevation; in addition, the visibility must also remain above three miles. All of this is another way of saying that an alternate must be filed in the flight plan if the weather forecast for your destination one hour before to one hour after is less than 2,000 feet and/or three miles visibility (See Fig. 3-1).

To illustrate it for memory purposes let's do it like this. This will help you remember both the fuel requirements and preflight action.

Fuel Requirements
Destination

+

Alternate

+

Anticipated Traffic Delays

+

45 Minutes at Normal Cruise

Total Fuel Required

That covers you entirely for answering questions on fuel requirements. Later, in flight planning, you will use this aid and add numbers.

Now, let's try a couple of sample questions on fuel requirements and locate the pitfalls. (R.T.F.Q.)

When an alternate airport is required, you must have sufficient fuel to complete the flight to the . . .

1. first airport of intended landing and fly to an alternate airport within 45 minutes at normal cruising speed.
2. first airport of intended landing, then to the alternate, then fly for 45 minutes at normal cruising speed.
3. alternate and fly thereafter for 45 minutes at normal cruising speed.
4. first airport of intended landing then to the alternate, then fly for 45 minutes at holding speed.

Choice No. 2 is most correct because it is a direct feedback of

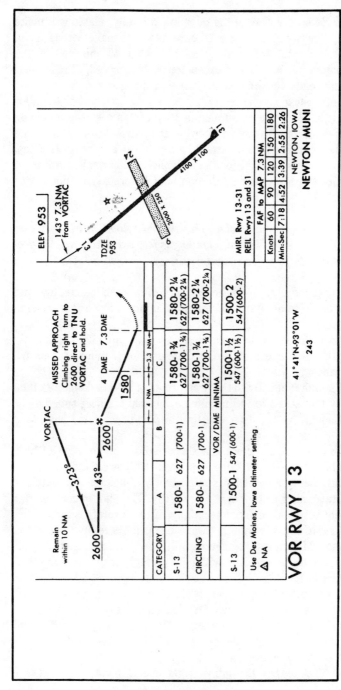

Fig. 3-1. For this airport, and alternate is required if the ceiling is less than 2,647 feet AGL. Also, note this airport is not available as an alternate.

39

91.23. Be sure you read the question carefully. Haste will make waste. The two errors the FAA expects you to make here is in No. 1 where it states the alternate is within 45 minutes of the destination. No. 4 is correct except for "holding speed." Remember, the rule reads 45 minutes at normal cruising speed.

The next question tests your knowledge of the 2,000 and/or three rule. With the revamping in 1979 of this rule, the following question becomes easy to answer. It is straightforward. If the weather is forecast to be less than 2,000 feet and/or three miles, you must consider fuel for the alternate. Additionally, you must consider the forecast period—one hour before to one hour after ETA.

What are the minimum fuel requirements for a flight in IFR conditions if the first airport of intended landing is forecast to have a 1,500-foot ceiling and three miles visibility at flight planned ETA?

1. Enough fuel to fly to the first airport of intended landing, and then fly to an alternate within 45 minutes at normal cruising speed.
2. Enough fuel to fly to the first airport of intended landing, fly to the alternate, and then fly thereafter for 45 minutes at normal cruising speed.
3. Enough fuel to fly to the first airport of intended landing, then fly thereafter for 45 minutes at normal cruising speed.
4. Enough fuel to fly to the first airport of intended landing.

Choice No. 2 is correct. It is almost a direct quote of FAR 91.23.

The next area of questions deals with preflight action for aircraft. Paragraph 91.29 is important yet simple. You may not operate an aircraft that is not airworthy. The pilot in command is entirely responsible for determining if the aircraft is airworthy. Needless to say, you wouldn't want to crash. Therefore, inherently, you should follow this regulation. Still, yearly, there are lots of fools that jump into an airplane without a preflight inspection and then pay dearly for it.

A few test questions deal with minimum equipment required for an instrument flight. The questions seem to dwell on navigational and radio equipment rather than the basic engine and directional gyro instrumentation. So, with respect to 91.33 let's dwell on radio equipment.

91.33 states that the radio navigation equipment, as well as two-way radio communications equipment, must be carried aboard the aircraft appropriate to the ground facilities to be used. In other words, if your proposed flight was cross-country to an airport with a VOR approach only, the flight could be made with just two-way radio equipment and a VOR receiver.

A new rule, and part of 91.33, is the transponder requirements. You now need transponders with Mode C capability above 12,500 feet. So, if you fly out west or where you are likely to fly at these altitudes, remember this one.

Ever since the Terminal Control Areas (TCA) were conceived, transponders have been needed to go into them. Group I TCAs require altitude reporting or Mode C capability. Group II TCAs require a transponder only. Note that Mode C means a coupled transponder with an encoding altimeter.

The Positive Control Area that starts at 18,000 (FL 180) requires some special equipment. That equipment is Distance Measuring Equipment, usually abbreviated DME.

The above mentioned equipment requirements should answer all of those kind of questions on the test. There was one that I uncovered in my research about the *vertical speed indicator*. The VSI is not a required piece of equipment. Therefore the question can be treated accordingly. Remember, the VSI is *not* required.

Here's a sample question on equipment requirements.

What minimum navigational equipment is required for IFR flight?

1. VOR, ADF, and ILS receivers.
2. Navigation equipment appropriate to the ground facilities used.
3. VOR receiver, transponder, and DME.
4. VOR receiver and, if in ARTS III environment, a coded transponder equipped for altitude reporting.

Choice No. 2 is the correct one. Once again, the answer is a direct quote from the regulations.

A fairly recent change in the FARs, particularly FAR 91.33, is the source of a new question on the written exam. The subject is the requirement of DME in the cockpit. In previous years, DME was a requirement of airplanes intending to operate in the Positive Control Area, those altitudes above 18,000 feet. This requirement has been changed to a 24,000-foot restriction if VOR ground facilities are to be used for navigation. Here's the question.

Where is DME required for instrument flight?

1. At or above 24,000 feet, MSL if VOR navigational equipment is required.
2. In positive control areas.
3. Above 18,000 feet MSL.
4. In the continental control area if VOR navigational equipment is used.

As you can see, if you are not informed on the latest regulation, you could answer this question incorrectly. You would probably choose either answer 2 or 3, which would be correct according to the old regulation; however, choice No. 1 is the correct response straight from 91.33 paragraph (e).

It is important to realize the FAA tends to jam questions with extraneous information. One such example:

Above what minimum altitude, excluding the airspace at and below 2,500 feet AGL, must airplanes and helicopters be equipped with operable transponders having Mode C capability when flying in controlled airspace of the 48 contiguous states?

1. 18,000 feet MSL
2. 14,000 feet MSL
3. 12,500 feet MSL
4. 10,000 feet MSL

Answer No. 3 is correct. Purely and simply a case of memory. To help you remember this, use this aid: the most common code squawked on a transponder is 1200. Thus 12 is the key. Transponders above 12,500 feet squawking 1200. Get it? That should keep that rule straight for you.

Other questions regarding navigation equipment center on VOR checks. There are four different types of checks. In order of preference of use they are: VOT test, ground check point, VOR comparison, and airborne check point. All checks may have an error of plus or minus four degrees, except the airborne check point, which allows six degrees either way.

One question in particular deals with the VOT test signal. To use the VOT, first the proper frequency must be tuned. (see Fig. 3- 2.) Then the OBS should be set to 180 degrees and the ambiguity meter should read a TO indication. The way to remember this is the airplane made by Cessna, the 182. Thus with a 180 degree OBS setting you should have a TO indication. The test can also be done

Fig. 3-2. The VOT check is the most accurate method for checking your VOR equipment. Notice the 180 degree TO.

with 360 degrees set as the radial with a FROM indication. As stated before, the allowable error with a VOT test is plus or minus four degrees.

A short mention here while discussing tests and equipment. The transponder and altimeter and static system must be checked every 24 months, however, not necessarily in the same 24 months.

Which checks and inspections of flight instruments or instrument systems must be accomplished before an airplane can be flown under IFR?

1. VOR within 30 days, altimeter systems within 24 calendar months, and transponder within 24 months.
2. ELT test within 30 days, altimeter systems within 12 calendar months, and transponder within 24 calendar months.
3. VOR within 24 calendar months, transponder within 24 calendar months, and altimeter system within 12 calendar months.
4. Airspeed indicator within 24 calendar months, altimeter system within 24 calendar months, and transponder within 12 calendar months.

The correct answer, based on FAR 91.171 and 91.172, is No. 1. I highly applaud the FAA for simplifying this regulation. Before, it was an exercise in legal double talk and almost everyone got it wrong.

We can all thank the FAA for simplifying the regulations. If you never were exposed to the instrument flying regulations prior to this, then you can praise the Lord! The one rule that has probably been simplified the most is the requirement for an alternate to be filed. As I discussed earlier, the weather must be forecast one hour before to one hour after our ETA to be lower than a ceiling of 2,000 feet and/or three miles visibility. Reviewing this doesn't hurt, but it does raise the question that if the destination airport requires a forecast, then doesn't the alternate require a minimum *good* forecast for use as an alternate? The answer is an emphatic yes!

One source of confusion is that the time period that the forecast must be valid is different for the alternate from the destination. Where the destination requires a time period from one hour before to one hour after, the alternate itself requires a forecast be valid for the ETA only. For purposes of testing, you should remember this rule. In actual operation, you will find that forecasts prepared for even your alternate will likely have as much as a four-hour time span.

Next, the naming of an alternate requires you to know what kind of approach(es) are available at the aerodrome. The regulation considers nonprecision approach minima as well as precision approach minima. For example, you plan a flight and name an alternate due to bad forecasts at your destination. The alternate you have chosen has only a VOR approach. The alternate minimums that apply for that airport (if no others are published) are a ceiling of at least 800 feet and two miles visibility. If the alternate has an ILS, then the required weather minima at ETA need only be a 600-foot ceiling and two statute miles visibility.

The way I remember these rules on alternates is to make catch phrases out of them. We know a nonprecision approach requires higher landing minimums. Therefore, the rule is "800 and two." For an ILS or PAR-equipped alternate, it is somewhat less: "600 and two." And if the alternate has no approach, the weather must be good enough to allow descent from the MEA, and you make the approach to the airport under basic VFR.

The availability of an alternate is described on the approach chart as shown in the figures. If the minimums published are other than the basic "800 and two" or "600 and two" rules, then those minimums apply. Before naming an alternate, one should check that he has that approach plate in his possession as well as the availability of it. The availability of an airport as an alternate depends on whether or not there is a terminal forecast for that airport. In general, you can say that airports having no Flight Service Station or weather reporting agency will not be available as an alternate. With the first airport of intended landing it is somewhat different. Under Part 91, a pilot may shoot an approach(es) to an airport that has no weather reporting.

Another interesting fact is the minimums for choosing an alternate no longer apply once the pilot has diverted to the alternate. If, for example, you had shot an approach and missed at your destination airport and had diverted toward your flight planned alternate and found the weather to be only "200 and one," you may continue to the alternate. This rule tends to confuse many because ordinarily you think of the alternate as having to be forecast to be "800 and two" or "600 and two." But when all the forecasts are going sour, including your alternate, one may continue on legally.

Here's the trickiest question the FAA has on alternates. Try your luck on this one:

When may an airport which does not have a published instrument approach be used as an alternate?

1. When the existing ceiling and visibility is at least 2,000 feet and three miles.
2. When the ceiling and visibility forecast for your ETA is at least 1,500 feet and five miles.
3. When the forecast ceiling and visibility from two hours before to two hours after your ETA is at least 1,000 feet and three miles.
4. When the ceiling and visibility minimums permit descent from the MEA, approach, and landing under basic VFR.

When using a destination airport not having a published instrument approach, descending to the MEA is the best one can do. No. 4 is the correct choice. I might add that if one needs to file IFR to get to a destination, the destination is as often as not obscured by some sort of instrument condition. On more than one occasion I have been disappointed at an out-of-the-way rural airport when, after descending to the MEA, I saw nothing but the inside of my windshield. It is a poor practice at best, but not dangerous if you stick right to the regs with it.

Moving on to other areas of flight planning, we come to Part

91.31. This regulation details the information each of us must be able to determine from instrument markings. These questions query on airspeed markings on the airspeed indicator. The questions ask things like what is the speed marked by the top of the white arc? The answers should be familiar to you from being a private pilot.

DEPARTURE REGULATIONS

Everyone is aware that the pilot in command has the final authority and decision in his hands with regard to the safety of the flight. The FAA will test this knowledge area as well as the regulation concerning deviation from the rules. Any pilot in command may deviate from any regulation in order to meet the emergency at hand. If a deviation is required by an unfortunate turn of events, certain reports are required.

In the event of an emergency, the pilot may deviate. If the pilot deviates from a clearance previously issued by ATC, he must notify ATC at first convenience. In declaring an emergency, the pilot and his aircraft gain priority over all other traffic. If the ATC so requests, however, the pilot must submit a written report within 48 hours to the chief of that ATC facility. So the rule is—"deviate if you must, explain if you're asked; 48 hours is all that is granted for the task."

Some of the other misfortunes that befall IFR pilots are radio malfunctions. Radio malfunctions, as might be expected, must also be reported. If a VOR, TACAN, ADF equipment, or low frequency navigation receiver becomes inoperative, ATC must be notified. Complete or partial loss of ILS receiver capability, as well as impairment of two-way radio communications, must be qualified with ATC. The proper method for notification to use is aircraft identification, equipment affected, degree of impairment, and assistance desired from ATC. These are all just ordinary common sense flying tips, but they are written down for your review in Part 91.

ENROUTE REGULATIONS

The bulk of the enroute regulations under Part 91 centers around the definitions of the following terms; MEA, MOCA, MCA, MRA, and MAA. At this point, I will take time to define these definitions in terms that apply to the type of questions the FAA is likely to throw at us.

Minimum Enroute Altitudes. The MEA is generally the

lowest altitude a pilot can fly on an IFR flight plan. The MEA guarantees 1,000 feet of clearance above the highest obstacle within five statute miles of the centerline of the airway. In mountainous terrain, the MEA guarantees 2,000 feet above the highest obstacle. In addition to providing obstruction clearance, the MEA is also set at an altitude that will give a usable navigation signal anywhere along the airway. If a pilot flies above the MEA, he'll be assured of terrain clearance and usable navigation signals. That's comfortable insurance when cruising through dense clouds at 150 or 200 miles per hour.

Minimum Obstruction Clearance Altitude. The MOCA guarantees terrain clearance, as does the MEA. The MOCA however, is always lower and only guarantees usable navigation signals within 22 nautical miles of the VOR facility.

Minimum Crossing Altitude. The MCA is a terrain clearance altitude that requires a pilot to cross certain fixes in order to be safely positioned, altitude-wise, with respect to terrain. For instance, if the terrain rises sharply ahead of you along your route, an MRA will almost certainly apply in order that you climb and arrive at that altitude before reaching the high terrain. By the same token, one may descend after crossing the MRA if travelling to a route segment having a lower MEA. (See Fig. 3-3.)

Minimum Reception Altitude. The MRA is the altitude which one must fly in order to receive the navigation signals forming an intersection or enroute fix. Usually this means the minimum reception altitude will be higher than the MEA. The VOR station forming a fix may be too far away or hidden by terrain at lower altitudes. Therefore, the need arises for an MRA.

Maximum Authorized Altitude. The MAA is established

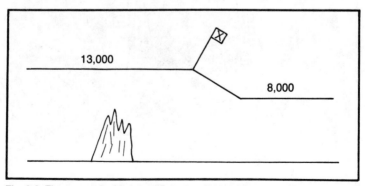

Fig. 3-3. The reason for Minimum Crossing Altitudes becomes apparent when examining this profile view.

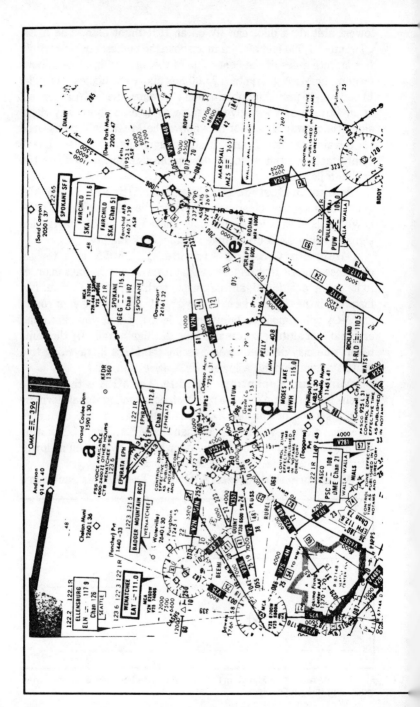

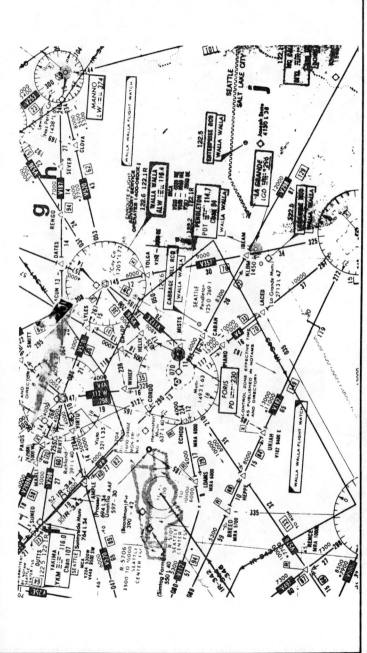

Fig. 3-4. Always consult the appropriate chart while taking the exam.

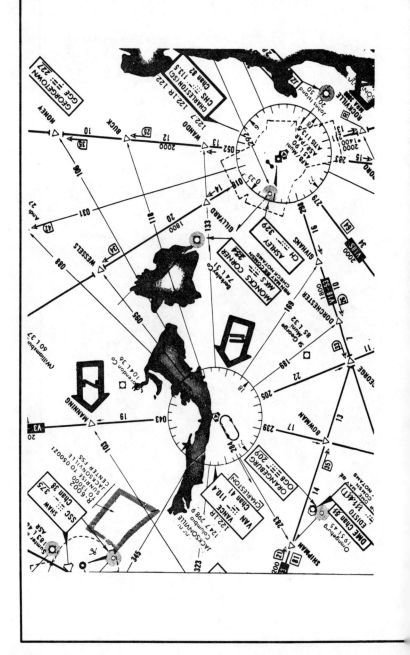

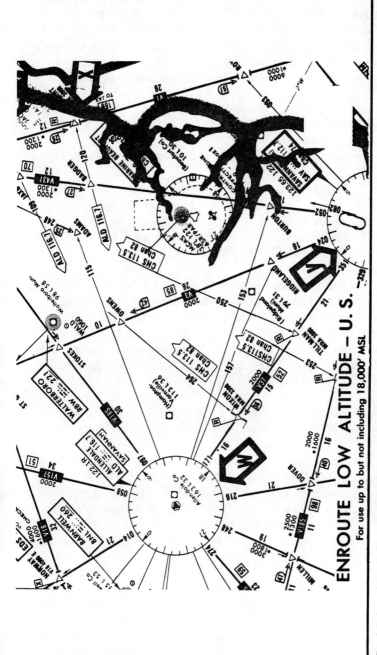

ENROUTE LOW ALTITUDE – U. S.

For use up to but not including 18,000' MSL

Fig. 3-5. Low Altitude Enroute Chart for the Charleston, S.C. Area.

in areas where a pilot may receive two VOR signals on the same frequency at the same time. There are a limited amount of VOR frequencies available. Therefore, it it possible in some places to climb high enough to receive two signals at once. The MAA is used to eliminate this problem. The pilot can then believe his VOR.

The following are some questions to examine and attack:

What is the purpose of the 6,000-foot MRA at RODNA Intersection (e)? (See Fig. 3-5.)

1. To provide an adequate altitude to receive GEG and PDT VORTACs.
2. To provide a high enough altitude for ATC radar coverage.
3. To provide a minimum altitude to receive navigation signals from EPH VORTAC.
4. To provide an adequate altitude to receive R-185 and DME signals from GEG VORTAC.

The reason for the high MRA near GEG VORTAC is not due to obstruction clearance, as one might believe at first. Realistically, the reason is that the intersection is made of the EPH 075 degree radial and the GEG 185 degree radial. Because the EPH VORTAC is at quite a distance, the MRA is due to that reason. I might also add that in real life flying that intersection may be identified by DME without tuning in EPH. Choice No. 3 is the correct answer.

What is the significance of the MRA at BAY POINT Intersection (x on Fig. 3-5)?

1. Navigation signals from both CHS and ALD are not adequate to identify BAY POINT below 3,000 feet.
2. The minimum altitude is 3,000 feet, which ensures adequate signal reception to identify BAY POINT without DME.
3. DME signal reception if unreliable below 3,000 feet.
4. The minimum altitude is 3,000 feet to identify BAY POINT by DME from CHS.

Once again, the key to these problems is knowing the definition by heart. The MRA, remember, refers only to the altitude needed to receive the VOR facility that forms the fix or intersection. Choice No. 1 is the only answer that addresses the definition at all.

You are planning a direct IFR flight from Airport A to Airport B on a magnetic course of 130 degrees in a nonmountainous area. Part of the route between A and B is out of controlled airspace. What is the minimum altitude you can fly for the part out of controlled airspace?

1. The altitude assigned by ATC.
2. An altitude at least 1,000 feet above the highest obstacle shown on a Sectional Chart within a horizontal distance of five statute miles from the course to be flown and an odd- thousand foot level MSL.
3. An altitude which is the highest MEA found within 10 nautical miles on either side of the route.
4. An altitude 1,000 feet above the highest obstacle shown on the Low Altitude Enroute Chart within a horizontal distance of 10 nautical miles of the route and an odd-thousand foot level MSL.

Part 91.121 defines the guidelines for flying IFR in uncontrolled airspace. The guideline follows precisely those set up for MOCAs on airways. Therefore, if you plan a flight across uncontrolled airspace, you are responsible for providing your own MOCA. Thus, by the definition, choice No. 2 becomes correct. Don't forget we fly odd-thousands going east and even-thousands going west, though at times ATC will occasionally abridge that rule when necessary.

Loss of communications occurs infrequently. When it does though, you would best have a plan of action in mind. Paragraph 91.127 lays out that plan of action. It is based on common sense and good operating principles. It states, if communication failure occurs in VFR conditions, you should continue the flight VFR and land as soon as practical. That makes sense doesn't it?

Loss of communications during IFR conditions is little more sticky but sensible. According to the FAA, you should continue along the last assigned route. What if you're being vectored? If communications loss occurs during this activity, they you should proceed direct to the fix, route, or airway specified in the vector clearance. For example, the controller will always say something like this, "This is vectors for the ILS runway 35 approach." The fix one would proceed to is the outer marker, in the event of loss of communications.

In the absence of an assigned route, you should continue along the route that ATC specified that you could expect in a further clearance. If none of these things are going your way, you can resort to your flight planned route.

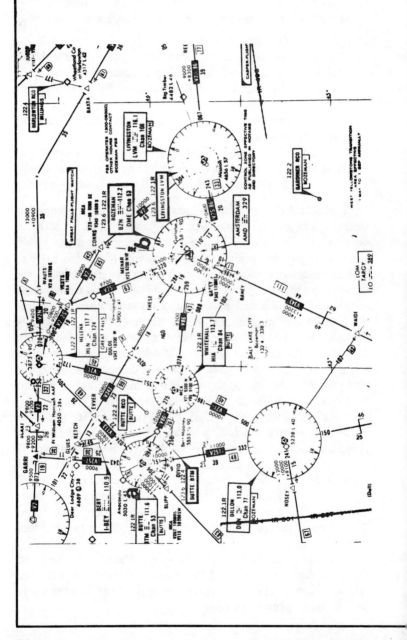

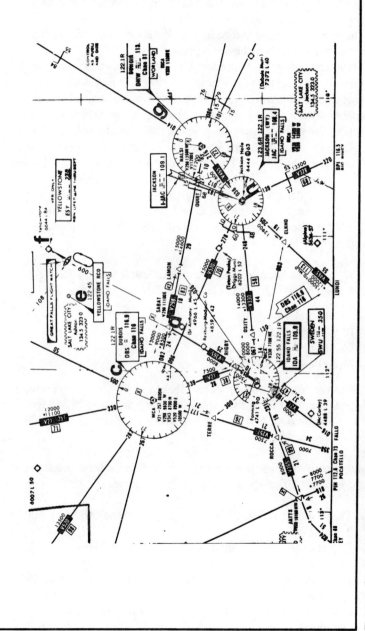

Fig. 3-6. Chart showing limiting cruising altitudes for a VFR-on-Top flight.

55

Once you have arrived at your destination, you must shoot an approach. However, you may not commence that approach until your expected clearance time or the ETA from your flight plan. If you arrive early, you must hold at the enroute altitude, which by the way, will be the last assigned altitude or the MEA for the last route segment whichever is higher.

If you have an expect approach clearance (EAC) time, you must cross over the final approach fix at that time. Timing is a bit more important than usual when you have no radios. In fact, it becomes almost everything. The only saving grace is that in most places the watchful eye of radar may be keeping the way cleared for you.

Recently, the FAA has chosen to explore the protocol for operating a flight VFR-on-Top. It should be understood that VFR-on-Top clearances are IFR flights operating at VFR altitudes. In other words, a flight must maintain altitude above the MEA and out of the clouds, because ATC will not provide separation of aircraft for the VFR-on-Top aircraft. Examine the following question.

What are the two limiting cruising altitudes usable for a VFR-on-Top flight from BZN VOR (b) to DBS VORTAC (c)? (See Fig. 3-6.)

1. 13,200 and 18,000 ft.
2. 14,000 and 18,000 ft.
3. 14,500 and 18,500 ft.
4. 14,500 and 16,500 ft.

Answer No. 4 is correct. The MEA is 14,000 feet, therefore, VFR-on-Top must fly at 14,500 west of north or south, 16,500 feet is also available. Due to the positive control area beginning at 18,000 feet, 18,500 feet is not available.

What is the minimum flight visibility and distance from clouds for flight at 10,500 ft. with a "VFR-on-Top" clearance?

1. Three statute miles, 1,000 ft. above, 500 ft. below, and 2,000 ft. horizontal.
2. Five statute miles, 1,000 ft. above, 1,000 ft. below, and 1 mile horizontal.
3. Three statute miles, 500 ft. above, 1,000 ft. below, and 2,000 ft. horizontal.
4. Five statute miles, 1,000 ft. above, 500 ft. below, and 1 mile horizontal.

If you have checked your FARs on this one, then you already know that 91.105 states that choice No. 2 is the correct answer.

What reports are required of a flight operating on an IFR clearance specifying VFR-on-Top in a nonradar environment?

1. The same reports that are required for any IFR flight.
2. All normal IFR reports except vacating altitudes.
3. All normal IFR reports except vacating altitudes and enroute position reports.
4. Only the reporting of any unforecast weather.

In the Airman's Information Manual, paragraph 341 states that regardless of the altitude or flight level being flown (including flights operating VFR-on-Top) pilots shall report over each reporting point used in the flight plan to define the route of flight. In other words, choice No. 1 is correct.

ARRIVAL REGULATIONS

The arrival regulations in Part 91 are not as explicit as other parts. Fundamentally, they lay down good operating practices that they expect pilots to follow.

Let's look at some questions and then explain them as they apply.

When should the turn to final approach be made on the teardrop procedure turn of the ILS RWY 5 approach at Fort Meyers? (Fig. 3-7.)

1. Execute the turn within 10 NM of the TCE NDB.
2. Beyond the 12 DME Arc.
3. Start the turn 12 miles from TCE NDB.
4. Start the turn immediately upon receiving a full off- course indication on the LOC.

The correct choice is No. 1. The approach should be followed as depicted. Most pilots and instructors agree that the approach and course reversal should be done in the most expeditious manner. One could follow the DME arc around, but the teardrop turn is faster and should be used for that reason.

A word about radar for guidance to the final approach fix: the rules in 91.116 are explicit as how to best use radar. The pilot must remain at the last assigned altitude given by ATC until established

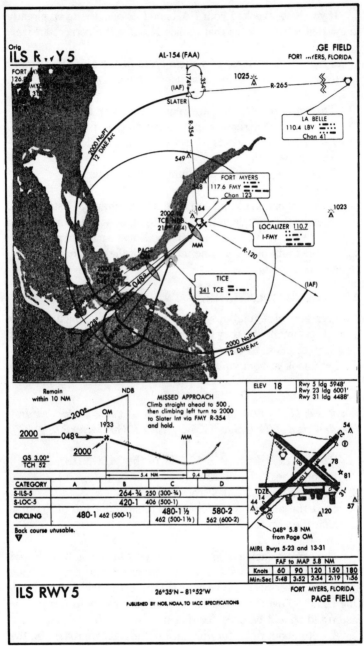

Fig. 3-7. Following a DME arc is one of the lesser known and lesser taught techniques on instrument flying.

on a published portion of the approach. Upon becoming established on the published portion of the approach, the altitudes published take precedence and can be followed.

If the approach is normal (if on an ILS), and the aircraft is in position for a normal approach, the pilot must execute a missed approach at the decision height if the runway or its environment is not visible. If the runway or its environment should disappear after reaching DH, the pilot should execute the missed approach procedures. An important point to remember is that the runway itself need not be in sight. Only the runway's environment has to be seen. That environment refers to the approach lighting system.

When must you initiate a missed approach procedure from an ILS approach if you are in position for a normal approach to the runway?

1. Only at the DH when the runway environment is not clearly visible.
2. Only after the time has expired after reaching the DH and the runway environment is not clearly visible.
3. Any time the runway environment is not visible after the time has expired after the FAF.
4. At the DH, if the runway or its environment is not clearly visible or any time thereafter that visual reference is lost.

Choice No. 4 is the only answer that accurately quotes 91.116. As with most of the FAA test questions on regulations, the correct answer is almost a direct quote from the rule book. Hence, it would be to every applicant's advantage to read the regulations.

Sometimes, equipment will decide to malfunction in accordance with Murphy's Law. In the event one is established on an ILS and the equipment malfunctions, the approach may be continued depending on what has become inoperative. For instance, if the glide slope receiver becomes inop inside the outer marker, the regulations specify that a pilot can complete the approach as a Localizer approach with higher minimums. As discussed earlier in the chapter, malfunctions need to be reported to ATC.

Understanding that the ILS is made up of the pilot's radio gear as well as the ground radio gear and approach lights is a key to some FAA test questions. The ILS is made up of five components. Those components are the Localizer, Glide Slope, Outer Marker, Middle Marker, and approach lighting system. Therefore, if any one or combination of those components becomes inoperative, then higher minimums apply. The following question, for instance, will explain better what is meant.

What are the DH and landing minimums for a straight-in ILS RWY 8R approach at Phoenix when the HIRL is inoperative? (See Fig. 3-8.)

1. 200 feet and 1/2 mile.
2. 1,312 feet and 1/2 mile.
3. 1,362 feet and 1/2 mile.
4. 1,362 feet and 1 mile.

Answer No. 2 is correct. But that is the normal DH and minimum landing visibility for a full ILS, you say! That is exactly correct. The small notation just above the profile view of the approach states "Inoperative table does not apply to HIRL RWY 8R." The rule here is as it is so many times in life— read the fine print. Many FAA questions that refer to approach plates will have the notations, which will be the answer, to the question. Questions on MDAs and DHs and procedure turns are particularly susceptible to this trick. Anytime that you refer to an approach plate, read *all* of it. Your score will jump 10 points just because you did. Guaranteed.

LDA approaches are seldom heard of and with good cause too. There are but four LDA approaches in the United States. An LDA approach is nothing more than a localizer approach, but the LDA localizer may be 90 degrees to the runway of intended landing, and the course may be twice as wide as the average ILS localizer. Nonetheless, the FAA is full of questions on SDFs and LDAs. SDF stands for "simplified directional approach," and is considered nonprecision. As a result, all such questions should be considered as nonprecision approaches, and that is all. That will keep things simplified for you.

To which minimum altitude may a pilot immediately descend upon being "cleared for approach" at BUXTON Intersection on the LDA BC RWY 8 approach at Pearson Airpark? (See Fig. 3-9.)

1. 3,400 feet.
2. 2,300 feet.
3. 2,700 feet.
4. 800 feet.

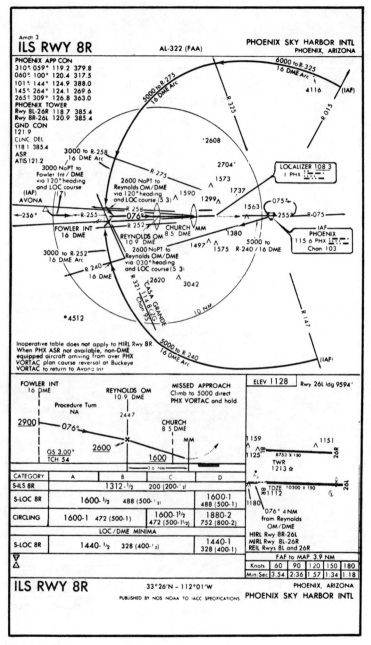

Fig. 3-8. The answer lies in the fine print of the Plan View.

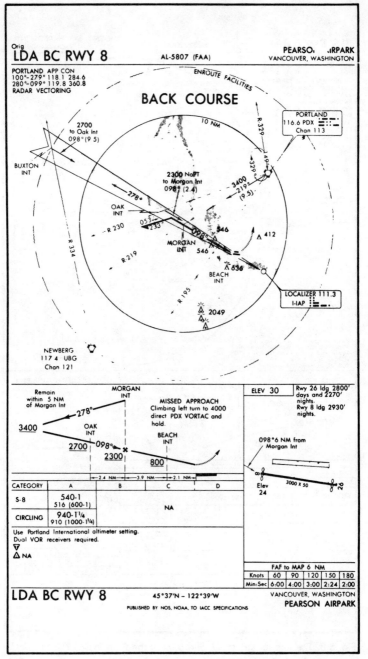

Fig. 3-9. This is one of the few LDA approaches in the United States.

Answer No. 1 is correct. Straight-in minimums apply after becoming established on the final approach course inside BUXTON.

Questions on landing minimums are bound to be encountered on the test. These usually refer to an approach plate. As we discussed earlier, reading the entire chart will be much to the benefit of the applicant, because so many times the answers are in the fine print. Understanding the number abbreviations for runway visual range will enable one to answer the questions accurately. Here is Table 3-1, straight from Part 91:

Obviously, there is no dark mystery to how the abbreviations are derived. Simply drop the last two zeros and there it is. Under pressure of test taking, however, when the figures such as 460/50 appear, applicants sometimes become confused. The number 460/50 stands for an MDA of 460 feet and a minimum landing visibility of 5,000 feet or 1 mile. The following question pertains to landing minimums. Let's see how well you can sail through it. All test questions on this subject are very similar.

What minimum weather conditions are required to execute a straight-in LOC BC RWY 11 approach and complete a landing at Oakland International? (See Fig. 3-10.)

1. 460-foot ceiling and 5,000 feet RVR.
2. 400-foot ceiling and 1 mile visibility.
3. Be able to see the runway environment when at MDA (360 feet).
4. 5,000 feet RVR.

Answer No. 1 is the correct choice, but it must be noted that 5,000 RVR is the only minimum that applies in order to commence

Table 3-1. Number Abbreviations for Runway Visual Range.

RVR	Equivalent Visibility	RVR Abbreviation
1600 feet	1/4 mile	16
2400 feet	1/2 mile	24
3200 feet	5/8 mile	32
4000 feet	3/4 mile	40
4500 feet	7/8 mile	45
5000 feet	1 mile	50
6000 feet	1/4 mile	60

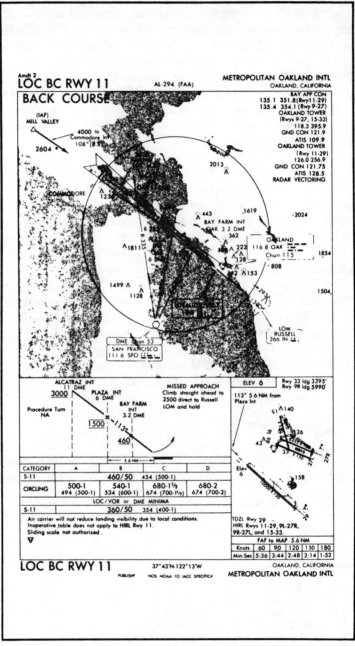

Fig. 3-10. Visibility is the only weather minimum that applies in order to begin the approach.

64

the approach; 460 feet is the MDA only. The trick is to RTFQ. The question asks what minimum weather condition to shoot the approach *and* complete a landing. Therefore, one must be able to descend below the clouds or ceiling to have the runway or its environment in sight before landing.

As in so many endeavors, if you know the pitfalls, avoiding them becomes easier. We have investigated the main areas of the FARs and the way the FAA approaches them in testing. The idea here was not to review every question and explain it. There are other sources of material that do that. The areas I covered are the areas of most difficulty to applicants for the Instrument Rating. Hopefully, you have been able to learn to see the target and avoid the barbs the FAA sets before you. After all, the FAA has no trick questions on the test. Just tricky ones.

Chapter 4

Instrument Navigation Charts

There are many good textbooks that outline and teach use of the instrument navigation charts. The purpose of this chapter is to point out the finer points of the charts as they apply to the Instrument Written exam. A legend is included at the rear of the chapter for your examination and reference.

ENROUTE CHARTS

The enroute chart, at first glance, appears to be a maze. There are, however, only five main things to know in order to answer questions on the written exam.

- The two numbers over the Victor airway symbol are minimum altitudes. The MEA and the MOCA. Which is which? The MOCA is always lowest and designated with an asterisk.
- The number in the letter"D" is the DME mileage. This distance on NOS charts is from the Vortac or compulsory reporting point. The best way to ensure a correct assumption is to add the two digit numbers below the Victor airway until they equal the "D" symbol. Then you will know what the origination is, a Vortac or a compulsory reporting point.
- The box with the letter "R" is a minimum reception altitude (MRA). This altitude is for the reception of off airway VORs or NDBs that form intersections. In other words, one must be at

that minimum altitude correctly identify the intersection.

- The box with the letter "X" is a minimum crossing altitude (MCA). This is for terrain clearance. Be careful with these. They may indicate a climb in one direction and a descent in the other. The descent is not necessarily mandatory but the climb is if your altitude is lower than the MCA.
- The square box under the Victor airway identification and to the right is the total mileage for the route segment between VORs.

What is the lowest altitude that assures acceptable navigation signal coverage at BOUNT and FOLSO Intersections for navigation outbound on V7E north of VULCAN VORTAC (d)? (See Fig. 4-1.) You are DME equipped.

1. 2,300 ft. at BOUNT; 3,000 ft. at FOLSO.
2. 3,000 ft. at BOUNT; 3,000 ft. at FOLSO.
3. 3,000 ft. at BOUNT; 7,000 ft. at FOLSO.
4. 4,000 ft. at BOUNT; 7,000 ft. at FOLSO.

Because you are DME equipped, you can use the lower MOCA at BOUNT. The MEA is necessary at FOLSO. Also, note that the reason you can use the MOCA at BOUNT is that it is only 22 miles from VULCAN, which ensures adequate navigation signal reception. All of this is another way of saying that No. 1 is the correct choice.

APPROACH CHARTS

The approach charts are easy to understand. The thing to know is where to look for important questions. For example, if a question was asked about a procedure turn, one looks at the plan view (the largest drawing, drawn to be viewed from the top) and checks the small print in the profile view. Referring to the ILS RWY 14R at Chicago O'Hare, you find that the procedure turn is deleted. It is deleted in the plan view and in fine print in the profile view is listed as NA or not applicable or unavailable.

Another possible question on this approach chart could be on the appropriate altitude to be flown at SEXXY Intersection. (See Fig. 4-2.) Let's assume the FAA asks that question. In this case the possible answers would be:

1. 5,000 feet only

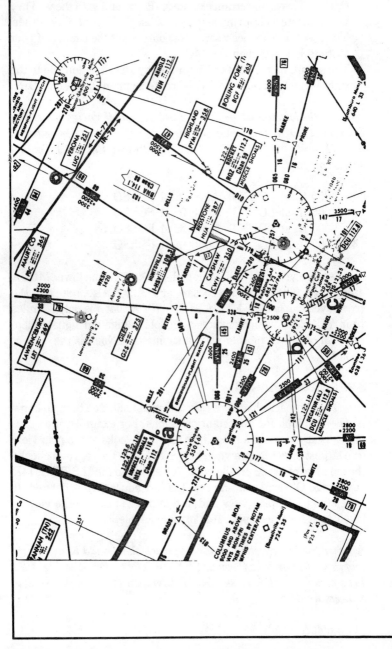

68

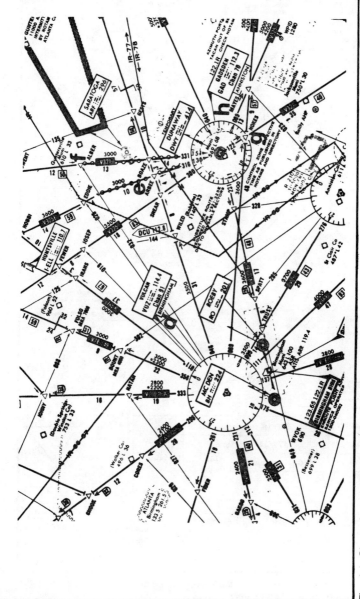

Fig. 4-1. Chart of southeastern United States flight paths.

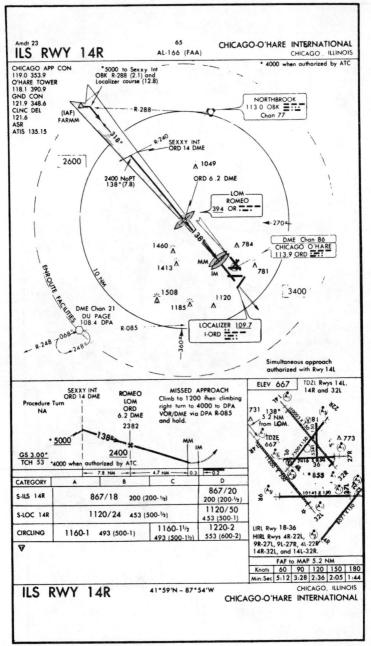

Fig. 4-2. Many times, the profile View must be consulted in order to fly the approach correctly and safely.

2. 4,000 feet when authorized by ATC
3. 2,400 feet when not using a procedure turn.
4. 2,600 feet.

The correct choice is not readily obvious. Looking at the plan view, you will find some fine print, which is asterisked and says 5,000 feet to SEXXY Intersection. The choice of "5,000 feet only" is incorrect because the asterisk says ATC can authorize 4,000 feet. The answer "2,400 with no PT" looks correct at first glance, but when examining the profile view, you will find that 2,400 feet is actually the altitude to cross ROMEO Intersection, which is the final approach fix. The "2,600- foot" answer is a catch for the hasty. The 2,600 stands for the minimum safe altitude in that area, which is displayed in the rectangular box to the left of SEXXY in the plan view. The only entirely correct choice is the "4,000 feet when authorized by ATC."

This is typical FAA thinking. It requires careful reading and some study of the entire approach chart. A helpful hint is to read the plan view first. I advise that one should read the plan view from left to right. Read all of the printed information regardless of whether it pertains to the question or not. It is protection. After studying the plan view, go to the profile view and read all of the printed information, then study the approach set up. Ordinarily, the questions will cause you to refer to the plan view, profile view, or the landing minimums chart. The bottom right-hand corner of the approach is reserved for the airport layout. All runways are depicted as taxiways. It is my opinion that this plan is not much use for knowing where to taxi when at a strange airport. Jeppesen does a much better job. The obvious questions, however, will be on the type of approach light system available at each runway. The symbols such as A_1, (see Fig. 4-3) are the denotation for approach light system type. On the test a legend would be provided. Then the task is only one of finding the right number. For instance, approach light system A_1 is the U.S. Standard. The approach lights are 3,000 feet in total length and high intensity. There are also sequence flashers installed. Once again, all of that information is available on the Approach Lighting Systems Legend.

Just above the landing minima chart is a division of categories. These divisions refer to aircraft approach speeds and maximum certificated landing weights. Different approach minimums are provided for different aircraft categories. Aircraft approach speed is established as 130 percent of the stall speed in the landing configura-

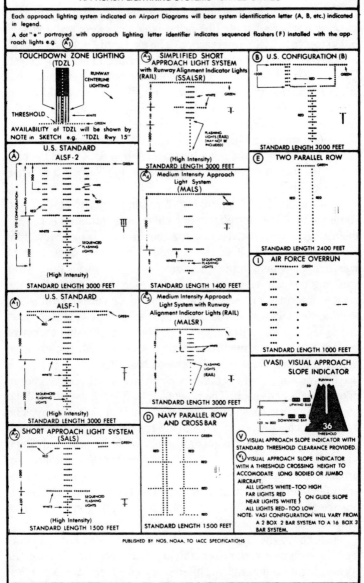

Fig. 4-3. It is next to impossible to remember all the variations on approach lights. That is why we should consult the legend.

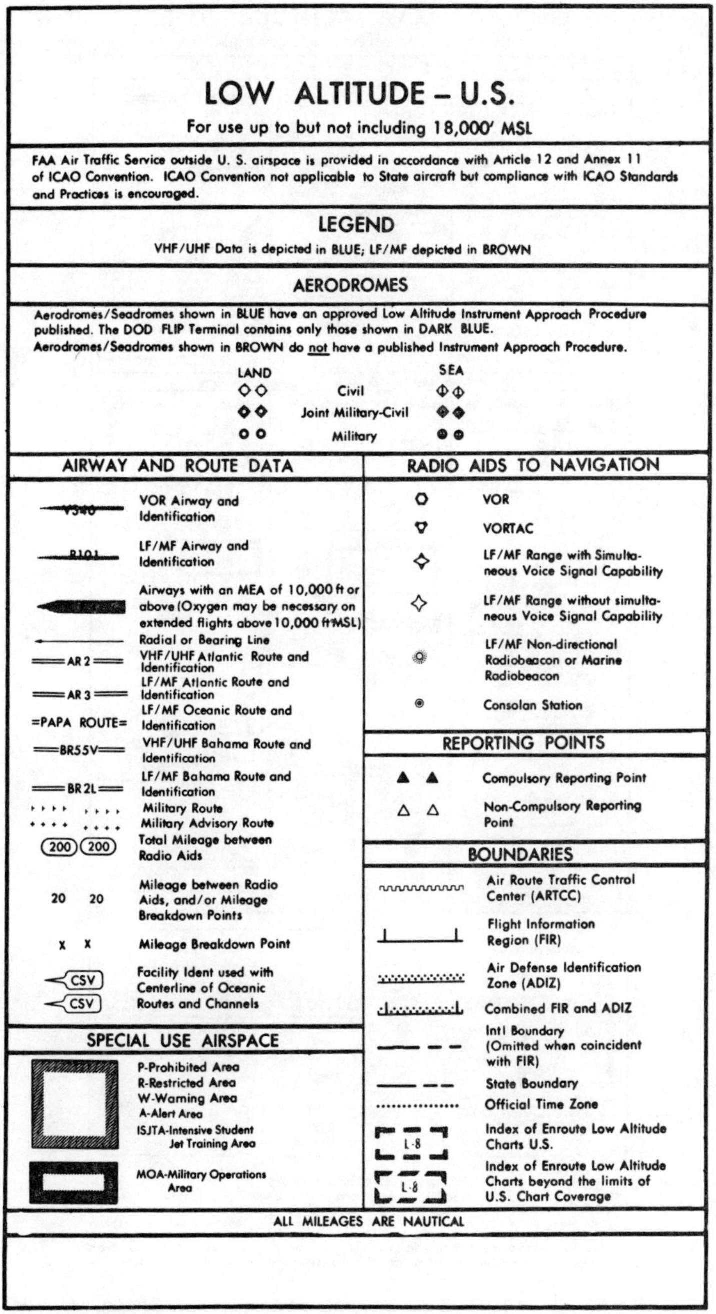

LOW ALTITUDE – U.S.

For use up to but not including 18,000' MSL

FAA Air Traffic Service outside U. S. airspace is provided in accordance with Article 12 and Annex 11 of ICAO Convention. ICAO Convention not applicable to State aircraft but compliance with ICAO Standards and Practices is encouraged.

LEGEND

VHF/UHF Data is depicted in BLUE; LF/MF depicted in BROWN

AERODROMES

Aerodromes/Seadromes shown in BLUE have an approved Low Altitude Instrument Approach Procedure published. The DOD FLIP Terminal contains only those shown in DARK BLUE.
Aerodromes/Seadromes shown in BROWN do not have a published Instrument Approach Procedure.

	LAND		SEA
◇ ◇		Civil	◈ ◈
◆ ◆		Joint Military-Civil	◉ ◉
○ ○		Military	● ●

AIRWAY AND ROUTE DATA

V340	VOR Airway and Identification
R101	LF/MF Airway and Identification
◀━━━	Airways with an MEA of 10,000 ft or above (Oxygen may be necessary on extended flights above 10,000 ft MSL)
━━▶	Radial or Bearing Line
═══ AR 2 ═══	VHF/UHF Atlantic Route and Identification
═══ AR 3 ═══	LF/MF Atlantic Route and Identification
=PAPA ROUTE=	LF/MF Oceanic Route and Identification
═══BR55V═══	VHF/UHF Bahama Route and Identification
═══ BR 2L ═══	LF/MF Bahama Route and Identification
▸ ▸ ▸ ▸ ▸ ▸ ▸ ▸	Military Route
✛ ✛ ✛ ✛ ✛ ✛ ✛ ✛	Military Advisory Route
(200)(200)	Total Mileage between Radio Aids
20 20	Mileage between Radio Aids, and/or Mileage Breakdown Points
x x	Mileage Breakdown Point
◀CSV ◀CSV	Facility Ident used with Centerline of Oceanic Routes and Channels

RADIO AIDS TO NAVIGATION

○	VOR
▽	VORTAC
◇	LF/MF Range with Simultaneous Voice Signal Capability
◇	LF/MF Range without simultaneous Voice Signal Capability
◎	LF/MF Non-directional Radiobeacon or Marine Radiobeacon
◉	Consolan Station

REPORTING POINTS

▲ ▲	Compulsory Reporting Point
△ △	Non-Compulsory Reporting Point

BOUNDARIES

∿∿∿∿∿	Air Route Traffic Control Center (ARTCC)
⌐_⌐_⌐	Flight Information Region (FIR)
⋯⋯⋯⋯	Air Defense Identification Zone (ADIZ)
⌐⋯⌐⋯	Combined FIR and ADIZ
— — —	Intl Boundary (Omitted when coincident with FIR)
— — —	State Boundary
⋯⋯⋯⋯⋯	Official Time Zone
⌐ ¬ L·8 ⌐ ¬	Index of Enroute Low Altitude Charts U.S.
⌐ ¬ L·8 L ⌐	Index of Enroute Low Altitude Charts beyond the limits of U.S. Chart Coverage

SPECIAL USE AIRSPACE

▨ (open box)	P-Prohibited Area R-Restricted Area W-Warning Area A-Alert Area ISJTA-Intensive Student Jet Training Area
▬ (filled box)	MOA-Military Operations Area

ALL MILEAGES ARE NAUTICAL

Fig. 4-4. Each type of chart has a legend that one should consult.

73

ENROUTE LOW ALTITUDE – U.S.

For use up to but not including 18,000' MSL

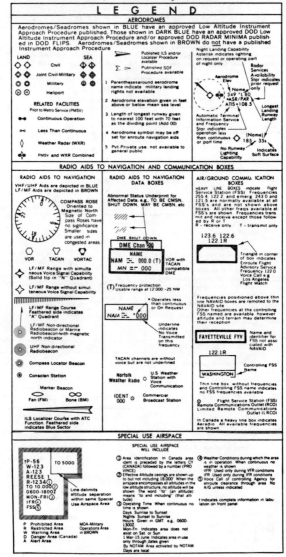

Fig. 4-5. Many of the symbols resemble those on Sectional Charts, which will make it easier to learn.

AIR TRAFFIC SERVICES AND AIRSPACE INFORMATION

AIRWAY AND ROUTE DATA

VHF/UHF Data is depicted in BLUE. LF/MF depicted in BROWN

V4 — VOR Airway and Identification

G3 — Airway and Identification

A RTE 10 — Uncontrolled Airway

BR 57V — Bahama Route and Identification

BR 10L — Bahama Route and Identification

AR 1 — Atlantic Route Identification

A15 ROUTE — Oceanic Route and Identification

▸ ▸ ▸ ▸ — Military IFR Route

• • • • — Flight Planning Route

-o-o-o-o-o- — Substitute Route Structure (See NOTAMS for facility outages) All relative and supporting data shown in brown

— Unusable or closed segment

V5 ∿∿∿ — Preferred Single Direction Airway

NME 000.0 — Facility Locator used with Radial Line in the formation of a Reporting Point

AME 000 — Facility Locator used with Bearing Line in the formation of a Reporting Point

REPORTING POINTS

▲ ▲ — Compulsory Reporting Point

△ △ — Non Compulsory Reporting Point

▲ ▲ — Offset Arrows indicate Facility Forming a Reporting Point Toward LF/MF and Away from VHF/UHF

BOUNDARIES

Ⓐ — Altimeter Setting Change

↔ — Altimeter Setting Change when not otherwise defined

— Air Route Traffic Control Center (ARTCC)

NAME / Name / 134 3 269 5 — ARTCC Remoted Sites with Discrete VHF and UHF Freqs

┄┄┄ — Flight Information Region (FIR)

┄┄┄ — Air Defense Identification Zone (ADIZ)

┄┄┄ — Combined FIR and ADIZ

- - - - Control Area (CTA)

- - - - Control Zone

╙╙╙ — Canadian Positive Control Zone

ⲦⲦⲦⲦ — Control Zones within which fixed wing special VFR flight is prohibited

— — Int'l Boundary (Omitted when coincident with ARTCC or FIR)

▬ ▬ — Area of Enlargement (Contains only data for through flights) See Area Charts for complete data

· · · · · Official Time Zone

→036→ — Radial Outbound from a UHF/VHF Radio Aid

—036→ — Bearing Inbound to a LF/MF Radio Aid

123 / **123** — Total Mileage between Compulsory Reporting Points and/or Radio Aids

23 / 23 — Mileage between other Reporting Points, Radio Aids, or/or Mileage Breakdown

42 / 26 — VOR Changeover Point Giving mileage to Radio Aids (Not shown at mid-point locations)

x x — Mileage breakdown

→ — Denotes DME fix (Distance same as route mileage)

15 — Denotes DME fix (Encircled mileage shown when not otherwise obvious)

MAA-15500 — MAA (Maximum Authorized Altitude)

3500 / 3500 — MEA (Minimum Enroute Altitude)

*3000 / *3000 — MOCA (Minimum Obstruction Clearance Altitude)

→EVEN — Canada only-Direction of Flight indicator (Shown when exception to Cruising Alt Diagram)

⊣ — MEA, MAA and/or MOCA Change at other than Radio Aids to Navigation

ℝ ℝ — MRA (Minimum Reception Altitude)

⚑ ⚑ — MCA (Minimum Crossing Altitude)

AIRSPACE INFORMATION

Open area (white) indicates controlled airspace
Shaded area (brown) indicates uncontrolled airspace up to 14,500'
THE BASE OF THE CONTINENTAL CONTROL AREA IS 14,500 FT MSL EXCLUDING THE AIRSPACE LESS THAN 1,500 FT ABOVE THE TERRAIN AND CERTAIN SPECIAL USE AIRSPACE AREAS

MISCELLANEOUS

┄┄┄ 1975 Isogonic Line and Value

ALL MILEAGES ARE NAUTICAL EXCEPT AS NOTED

ALL RADIALS AND BEARINGS ARE MAGNETIC

ALL ALTITUDES ARE MSL UNLESS OTHERWISE STATED

ALL TIME IS GREENWICH MEAN (STANDARD TIME) (GMT)

DAYS ARE LOCAL

‡DURING PERIODS OF DAYLIGHT SAVING TIME (DT) EFFECTIVE HOURS WILL BE ONE HOUR EARLIER THAN SHOWN

ALL CONTERMINOUS STATES ON DT EXCEPT ARIZONA AND THAT PORTION OF INDIANA IN THE EASTERN TIME ZONE

CRUISING ALTITUDES - U.S.

IFR EVEN Thousands	IFR ODD Thousands
VFR or ON TOP EVEN Thousands Plus 500'	VFR or ON TOP ODD Thousands Plus 500'

VFR above 3000' AGL
IFR Outside controlled airspace
IFR within controlled airspace as assigned by ATC
All courses are magnetic

EXAMPLE OF GROUPING

MEA is established where a gap in navigation signal coverage

Airway Restriction (Airway penetrates Special Use Airspace)

R-1234

MAA-15500 / 4000 / *3500

V30 / 54

NAME / MRA 4000

Holding Pattern

4000 / 3500 / V30 / 18 — MEA GAP

NAME / MCA 4000

4000 / 3000 / 3500 / A8 / 21

CONTROL 1148 FEET / ABOVE 2000 FEET

Water Vignette

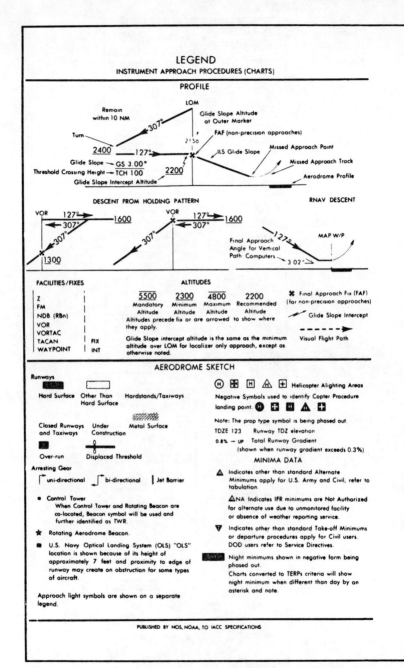

LEGEND
INSTRUMENT APPROACH PROCEDURES (CHARTS)

PROFILE

Remain within 10 NM

Turn

LOM

307°

Glide Slope Altitude at Outer Marker

2156

FAF (non-precision approaches)

2400

127°

ILS Glide Slope

Missed Approach Point

Missed Approach Track

Glide Slope — GS 3.00°

Threshold Crossing Height — TCH 100

2200

Aerodrome Profile

Glide Slope Intercept Altitude

DESCENT FROM HOLDING PATTERN

VOR 127° 1600

307°

307°

1300

VOR 127° 1600

307°

307°

RNAV DESCENT

Final Approach Angle for Vertical Path Computers

127°

MAP W/P

3 02°

FACILITIES/FIXES

Z
FM
NDB (RBn)
VOR
VORTAC
TACAN
WAYPOINT

FIX
INT

ALTITUDES

5500	2300	4800	2200
Mandatory Altitude	Minimum Altitude	Maximum Altitude	Recommended Altitude

Altitudes precede fix or are arrowed to show where they apply.

Glide Slope intercept altitude is the same as the minimum altitude over LOM for localizer only approach, except as otherwise noted.

✱ Final Approach Fix (FAF) (for non-precision approaches)

Glide Slope Intercept

- - - - - ▸ Visual Flight Path

AERODROME SKETCH

Runways

Hard Surface   Other Than Hard Surface   Hardstands/Taxiways

Closed Runways and Taxiways   Under Construction   Metal Surface

Over-run   Displaced Threshold

Arresting Gear

uni-directional   bi-directional   Jet Barrier

● Control Tower
When Control Tower and Rotating Beacon are co-located, Beacon symbol will be used and further identified as TWR.

★ Rotating Aerodrome Beacon.

■ U.S. Navy Optical Landing System (OLS) "OLS" location is shown because of its height of approximately 7 feet and proximity to edge of runway may create on obstruction for some types of aircraft.

Approach light symbols are shown on a separate legend.

Ⓗ ✛ Ⓗ ⚠ ✛ Helicopter Alighting Areas

Negative Symbols used to identify Copter Procedure landing point. Ⓗ ✛ Ⓗ ⚠ ✛

Note: The prop type symbol is being phased out.

TDZE 123   Runway TDZ elevation

0.8% — up   Total Runway Gradient
(shown when runway gradient exceeds 0.3%)

MINIMA DATA

△ Indicates other than standard Alternate Minimums apply for U.S. Army and Civil, refer to tabulation.

△NA Indicates IFR minimums are Not Authorized for alternate use due to unmonitored facility or absence of weather reporting service.

▽ Indicates other than standard Take-off Minimums or departure procedures apply for Civil users. DOD users refer to Service Directives.

Night minimums shown in negative form being phased out.
Charts converted to TERPs criteria will show night minimum when different than day by an asterisk and note.

PUBLISHED BY NOS, NOAA, TO IACC SPECIFICATIONS

Fig. 4-6. You will probably need to use approach charts more often than any other instrument chart. This legend will help you become familiar with them.

LEGEND
INSTRUMENT APPROACH PROCEDURES (CHARTS)

PLANVIEW SYMBOLS

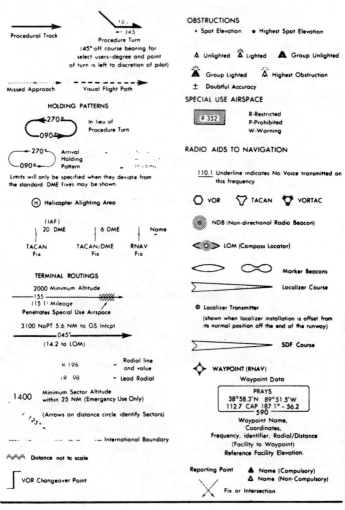

Procedural Track

Procedure Turn
(45° off course bearing for
select users—degree and point
of turn is left to discretion of pilot)

Missed Approach   Visual Flight Path

HOLDING PATTERNS

270°
090°   In lieu of
              Procedure Turn

270°   Arrival
090°   Holding
              Pattern

Limits will only be specified when they deviate from
the standard. DME fixes may be shown.

(H) Helicopter Alighting Area

(IAF)
20 DME   6 DME   Name
TACAN   TACAN/DME   RNAV
Fix   Fix   Fix

TERMINAL ROUTINGS

2000 Minimum Altitude
155
(15) Mileage
Penetrates Special Use Airspace

3100 NoPT 5.6 NM to GS Intcpt
045°
(14.2 to LOM)

R 198   Radial line
              and value
R 98   Lead Radial

1400   Minimum Sector Altitude
              within 25 NM (Emergency Use Only)

125°   (Arrows on distance circle identify Sectors)

International Boundary

Distance not to scale

VOR Changeover Point

OBSTRUCTIONS

• Spot Elevation   ● Highest Spot Elevation

△ Unlighted   △ Lighted   ▲ Group Unlighted

▲ Group Lighted   ▲ Highest Obstruction

± Doubtful Accuracy

SPECIAL USE AIRSPACE

R 352   R-Restricted
         P-Prohibited
         W-Warning

RADIO AIDS TO NAVIGATION

110.1 Underline indicates No Voice transmitted on
      this frequency

○ VOR   ▽ TACAN   ◇ VORTAC

NDB (Non-directional Radio Beacon)

LOM (Compass Locator)

Marker Beacons

Localizer Course

◎ Localizer Transmitter
(shown when localizer installation is offset from
its normal position off the end of the runway)

SDF Course

◇ WAYPOINT (RNAV)
Waypoint Data

PRAYS
38°58.3'N 89°51.5'W
112.7 CAP 187.1° – 56.2
590

Waypoint Name,
Coordinates,
Frequency, identifier, Radial/Distance
(Facility to Waypoint)
Reference Facility Elevation.

Reporting Point   ▲ Name (Compulsory)
                  △ Name (Non-Compulsory)
                  ✕ Fix or Intersection

PUBLISHED BY NOS, NOAA, TO IACC SPECIFICATIONS

LEGEND
STANDARD INSTRUMENT DEPARTURE (SID) CHARTS

RADIO AIDS TO NAVIGATION

○ VOR   ▽ TACAN   ▽ VORTAC

◇ WAYPOINT (RNAV)

⬡ NDB (Non-directional Radio Beacon)

◇ RANGE (Simultaneous Voice)

◇ RANGE (Non-Simultaneous Voice)

◉ LOM (Compass Locator)

◯◯◯ MARKER BEACONS

◁ LOCALIZER COURSE

AERODROMES

▭   ✳

Ⓗ Helicopter

RUNWAYS

▰ Hardsurface

▨ Metal Surface

▭ Closed

⋯⋯ Under Construction

▭ Other Than Hard Surface

⬚ Over-run / Hardstands / Taxiways

ROUTES

⟵ Departure Route

⟵ Transition Route

SPECIAL USE AIRSPACE

▨ R-5

R-Restricted
P-Prohibited
W-Warning
A-Alert

MISCELLANEOUS SYMBOLS

✕ △ Intersections

▲ Compulsory Reporting Point

| DME Fix

←R-275— Radial line and value

〰 Distance Not To Scale

⌐_⌐ Arresting Gear

▌ Jet Barrier

⦚ Displaced Threshold

■ Control Tower

0 8% DOWN ⟶ Take Off Gradient

⌐ Changeover Point

V-25 Airway Identification

Outer Marker (OM)-continuous dashes
Middle Marker (MM)-alternate dots and dashes.
<u>117.6</u>-frequency underlined indicates no voice capability.
All radials/bearings are magnetic.
All mileages are nautical.
Runway dimensions in feet.
Elevation in feet-MSL.

Fig. 4-7. SIDs and STARs were invented to relieve Air Traffic Controllers of a significant amount of work in congested terminal areas.

LEGEND

STANDARD TERMINAL ARRIVAL ROUTE (STAR) CHARTS

RADIO AIDS TO NAVIGATION

- ○ VOR
- ▽ TACAN
- ♈ VORTAC
- ◆ WAYPOINT (RNAV)
- ◇ RANGE (Simultaneous Broadcast)
- ⦿ NDB (Non-directional Radio Beacon)
- < ○ > LOM (Compass Locator)
- ⬡ Marker Beacons
- ◁ Localizer Course
- ◁ SDF Course

NAME
000 0 NAM 00 — DME or TACAN Channel

Underline indicates no voice transmitted on this frequency

← R-275 -- Radial line and value

Reporting Point
- △ Non-Compulsory
- ▲ Compulsory

DME Fix → 15 DME Mileage (when not obvious)

⌐ VOR Changeover Point

ROUTES

4500 MEA
* 3500 MOCA
←270°━━ Arrival Route
(65) Mileage

← Transition Route

⚑ MCA (Minimum Crossing Altitude)

x Mileage Breakdown

⊸ Altitude change at other than Radio Aids

(65) Mileage between Radio Aids, Reporting Points and Route Breaks

V12 J80 Airway/Route Identification

◯ Holding Pattern

SPECIAL USE AIRSPACE

R-352
- R-Restricted
- P-Prohibited
- W-Warning
- A-Alert

AERODROMES

- ◇ Civil
- ◆ Joint Civil-Military
- ◉ Military
- Ⓗ Heliport

Entry facility/fix identified by name and symbol only.
All radials/bearings are magnetic
All mileages are nautical
All altitudes in feet—MSL
MEA – Minimum Enroute Altitude
MOCA – Minimum Obstruction Clearance Altitude

tion. This is usually expressed as 1.3 V_{SO}. Category A is the lowest category. Is in fact possible for an aircraft to meet the qualifications of two different categories. In that case, the highest category must apply. Below is a reproduction of landing categories in chart form (Table 4-1).

Another fine point on an approach chart is the time to missed approach. This chart is shown below the airport layout in the bottom right-hand corner. The chart list various ground speeds from 60 to 190 knots. It should be pointed out that it is each pilot in command's duty before approach to get the winds at the airport and estimate his groundspeed on final approach in order to know the elapsed time from the final approach fix to the missed approach point.

Also, in the profile view in the lower left-hand corner is some important information—the inclination of the glide slope. In this case it is 3 degrees (ILS RWY 14R O'Hare). Directly below that information is TCH 53: Threshold Crossing Height is 53 feet. In addition, there in the lower left-hand corner of the entire chart is a letter "T" in a triangle. This means that other than standard take-off minimums apply. If it should also have an "A" in a triangle, other than standard alternate minimums apply. This information can be found in the alternate and take off minimums chart at the beginning of the NOS approach plate book. Reference to these type questions on the test will be provided. See Figs. 4-4 through 4-9.

Table 4-1. Aircraft Landing Categories.

Aircraft Category	Speed	Landing Weight
A	Less than 91 Knots	30,000 lbs. or less
B	91 to 120 Knots	30,001 to 60,000 lbs.
C	121 to 140 Knots	60,001 to 150,000 lbs.
D	141 to 165 Knots	150,001 lbs. or more

Instrument Approach Procedures (Charts)
INOPERATIVE COMPONENTS OR VISUAL AIDS TABLE
Civil Pilots see FAR 91.117(c)

Landing minimums published on instrument approach procedure charts are based upon
full operation of all components and visual aids associated with the particular instrument
approach chart being used. Higher minimums are required with inoperative components
or visual aids as indicated below. If more than one component is inoperative, each minimum is raised to the highest minimum required by any single component that is inoperative. ILS glide slope inoperative minim .ms are published on instrument approach charts
as localizer minimums. This table may be amended by notes on the approach chart. Such
notes apply only to the particular approach category(ies) as stated. See legend page for
description of components indicated below.

(1) ILS, MLS, and PAR

Inoperative Component or Aid	Approach Category	Increase DH	Increase Visibility
MM*	ABC	50 feet	None
MM*	D	50 feet	¼ mile
ALSF 1 & 2, MALSR, & SSALR	ABCD	None	¼ mile

*Not applicable to PAR

(2) ILS with visibility minimum of 1,800 or 2,000 RVR.

MM	ABC	50 feet	To 2400 RVR
MM	D	50 feet	To 4000 RVR
ALSF 1 & 2, MALSR, & SSALR	ABCD	None	To 4000 RVR
TDZL, RCLS	ABCD	None	To 2400 RVR
RVR	ABCD	None	To ½ mile

(3) VOR, VOR/DME, VORTAC, VOR (TAC), VOR/DME (TAC), LOC, LOC/DME,
LDA, LDA/DME, SDF, SDF/DME, RNAV, and ASR

Inoperative Visual Aid	Approach Category	Increase MDA	Increase Visibility
ALSF 1 & 2, MALSR, & SSALR	ABCD	None	½ mile
SSALS, MALS & ODALS	ABC	None	¼ mile

(4) NDB

ALSF 1 & 2, MALSR, & SSALR	C	None	½ mile
	ABD	None	¼ mile
MALS, SSALS, ODALS	ABC	None	¼ mile

14 APRIL 1977   PUBLISHED BY NOS. NOAA TO IACC SPECIFICATIONS

Fig. 4-8. When certain components of an instrument approach system are
inoperative, higher landing minimums may apply. You may have to check this
legend in flight.

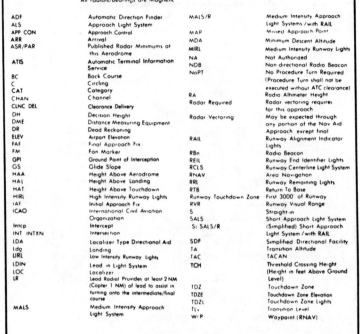

LEGEND
INSTRUMENT APPROACH PROCEDURES (CHARTS)

GENERAL INFORMATION & ABBREVIATIONS

★ Indicates control tower operates non-continuously
All distances in nautical miles (except Visibility Data which is in statute miles and Runway Visual Range which is in hundreds of feet)
Runway dimensions in feet
Elevations in feet Mean Sea Level
All radials/bearings are Magnetic

ADF	Automatic Direction Finder	MALS/R	Medium Intensity Approach Light Systems /with RAIL
ALS	Approach Light System		
APP CON	Approach Control	MAP	Missed Approach Point
ARR	Arrival	MDA	Minimum Descent Altitude
ASR/PAR	Published Radar Minimums at this Aerodrome	MIRL	Medium Intensity Runway Lights
		NA	Not Authorized
ATIS	Automatic Terminal Information Service	NDB	Non-directional Radio Beacon
		NoPT	No Procedure Turn Required (Procedure Turn shall not be executed without ATC clearance)
BC	Back Course		
C	Circling		
CAT	Category		
CHAN	Channel	RA	Radar Altimeter Height
CLNC DEL	Clearance Delivery	Radar Required	Radar vectoring required for this approach
DH	Decision Height		
DME	Distance Measuring Equipment	Radar Vectoring	May be expected through any portion of the Nav Aid Approach except final
DR	Dead Reckoning		
ELEV	Airport Elevation		
FAF	Final Approach Fix		
FM	Fan Marker	RAIL	Runway Alignment Indicator Lights
GPI	Ground Point of Interception		
GS	Glide Slope	RBn	Radio Beacon
HAA	Height Above Aerodrome	REIL	Runway End Identifier Lights
HAL	Height Above Landing	RCLS	Runway Centerline Light System
HAT	Height Above Touchdown	RNAV	Area Navigation
HIRL	High Intensity Runway Lights	RRL	Runway Remaining Lights
IAF	Initial Approach Fix	RTB	Return To Base
ICAO	International Civil Aviation Organization	Runway Touchdown Zone	First 3000' of Runway
		RVR	Runway Visual Range
Intcp	Intercept	S	Straight-in
INT INTXN	Intersection	SALS	Short Approach Light System
LDA	Localizer Type Directional Aid	Si SALS/R	(Simplified) Short Approach Light System /with RAIL
Ldg	Landing		
LIRL	Low Intensity Runway Lights	SDF	Simplified Directional Facility
LDIN	Lead in Light System	TA	Transition Altitude
LOC	Localizer	TAC	TACAN
LR	Lead Radial Provides at least 2 NM (Copter 1 NM) of lead to assist in turning onto the intermediate/final course	TCH	Threshold Crossing Height (Height in feet Above Ground Level)
		TDZ	Touchdown Zone
		TDZE	Touchdown Zone Elevation
MALS	Medium Intensity Approach Light System	TDZL	Touchdown Zone Lights
		TLv	Transition Level
		W/P	Waypoint (RNAV)

LANDING MINIMA FORMAT

In this example airport elevation is 1179, and runway touchdown zone elevation is 1152

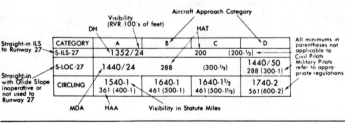

CATEGORY	A	B	C	D	
S-ILS-27	1352/24		200	(200-½)	
S-LOC-27	1440/24	288		(300-½)	1440/50 288 (300-1)
CIRCLING	1540-1 361 (400-1)	1640-1 461 (500-1)	1640-1½ 461 (500-1½)	1740-2 561 (600-2)	

Straight-in ILS to Runway 27
Straight-in with Glide Slope inoperative or not used to Runway 27

DH — Visibility (RVR 100's of feet) — Aircraft Approach Category — HAT

All minimums in parentheses not applicable to Civil Pilots Military Pilots refer to appropriate regulations

MDA — HAA — Visibility in Statute Miles

PUBLISHED BY NOS, NOAA, TO IACC SPECIFICATIONS

Fig. 4-9. The codes for landing minimums are explained well in this legend, and they should be committed to memory.

Chapter 5

Radio Orientation

One of the best ways to lose points on the instrument written exam is to become confused with radio orientation problems. I will discuss some methods in which to keep things in order and then examine representative questions from the exam.

The types of radio navigation used for testing purposes are the same as will be used in your instrument flying. Those are VOR, RMI, ADF, DME, and RNAV. The FAA likes to mix them up to keep you on your toes. Probably the least explained of all of these instruments is the RMI. It seems that many text books ignore its existence or fall short of the mark in explaining it to most students' satisfaction.

The RMI stands for *Radio Magnetic Indicator*. The name should remind one of what it actually does. The instrument is actually an ADF superimposed over a directional gyro. The beauty of this arrangement is clear once one understands what it simplifies. In using an everyday run-of-the-mill ADF to find the magnetic bearing (magnetic course) to the station, one must add and subtract, multiply and divide, to get the answer in accordance with the formula: MH (Magnetic Heading) + RB (Relative Bearing) = MB (Magnetic Bearing). Though this may be a simple matter while sitting in an easy chair at the house, in a tight approach situation I don't like to be doing arithmetic. I'll bet you don't either. The RMI steps in and simplifies an approach or tracking to a beacon or VOR station. When the pointer on an RMI points to 243 degrees for instance,

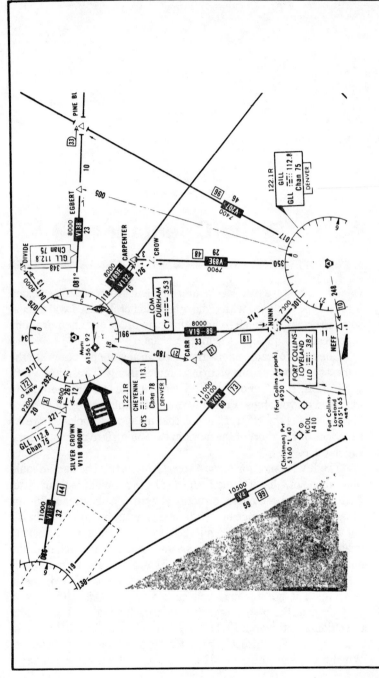

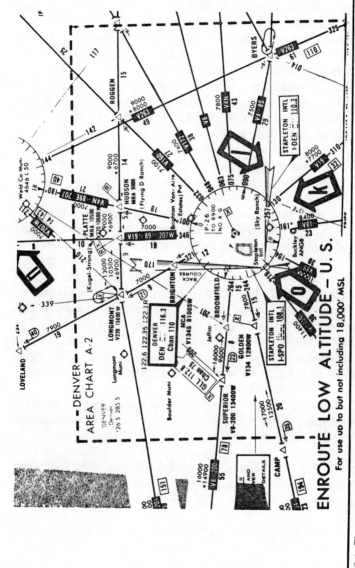

Fig. 5-1. The enroute chart for the Denver area.

the magnetic bearing to the station is 243 degrees. That's all there is to it. You just read directly from the needle.

What many textbooks fail to explain is that on many RMIs there are two needles. The needle with the single shaft is always tuned to the ADF station. The needle that has the double shaft is usually tuned to the number two VOR station. At least, for testing purposes, the needles are selected this way. Actually, it could also represent another NDB station. How does the needle select a VOR radial? It doesn't. It only points *at* the station as does the ADF. That is all! If the double shafted needle is pointing to the left or right of your track, then you may assume the VOR lies in that direction. Plainly and simply, the double shafted needle is a VOR station being displayed as an ADF. I will discuss the RMI further when examining some sample questions.

One of the hardest parts of orientation is to find oneself in relation to an intersection. Rule No. 1 should be, when dealing with VOR signals that form an intersection on an airway, the VOR ambiguity meter will always read FROM. Always! Once that is absorbed, the next rule will clear the muddy water on orientation. If the CDI (Course Deviation Indicator) is deflected to right and the VOR station that forms the intersection is also to the right of the aircraft, then the aircraft has not yet reached the intersection. And conversely, if it is to the left side of the aircraft and the CDI is to the left, then the aircraft is not yet to the intersection.

Once again, to make this clear, I will use another example. This time the VOR station is to the right and the CDI is to the left. The indication will be that the aircraft is past the intersection. In a nutshell, when an aircraft is past an intersection, the CDI will swing away from the VOR station. The ambiguity meter, as emphasized before, will read FROM.

Following through, we will examine some questions from the FAA written test to make it more clear and to practice for the real thing. Try this one.

Refer to Fig. 5-1. What is your position relative to V19 and NEFF Intersection (n) while proceeding from Denver VORTAC (k) to Cheyenne VORTAC (m) along V19? (See Fig. 5-2.)

1. Right of course, approaching NEFF Intersection.
2. Left of course, past NEFF Intersection.
3. Right of course, past NEFF Intersection.
4. Left of course, approaching NEFF Intersection.

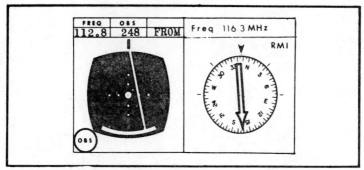

Fig. 5-2. VOR and RMI heads for reference.

In order to answer questions of this kind correctly, it is of great importance to check what VOR stations and radials are represented by the depictions. The frequency 112.8 and 248 degree radial belongs to Gill VOR, and that set up forms NEFF Intersection on V19. The RMI is set to Stapleton VOR at 116.3 MHz. The needle indicates that the 346-degree radial is to the right. You know this because the magnetic heading is 346 degrees, and the pointer will point to the side of the aircraft that the course is on. It indicated to the right, therefore, the aircraft is left of course.

Following my rule, if the VOR station is to the right of the airway and the CDI is to the right, then you have not yet reached the intersection. Putting your two deductions together, you will find that choice No. 4 is the only correct one.

If you are still confused, here is another way to orient oneself to the VOR station. In the figure is an aid anyone can draw quickly. The top of the arrow represents the OBS or the magnetic course. The top half of the aid is the FROM envelope and the bottom half

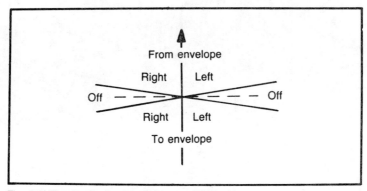

Fig. 5-3. The handy-dandy, all-purpose, VOR aid.

ENROUTE LOW ALTITUDE – U.S.

For use up to but not including 18,000' MSL

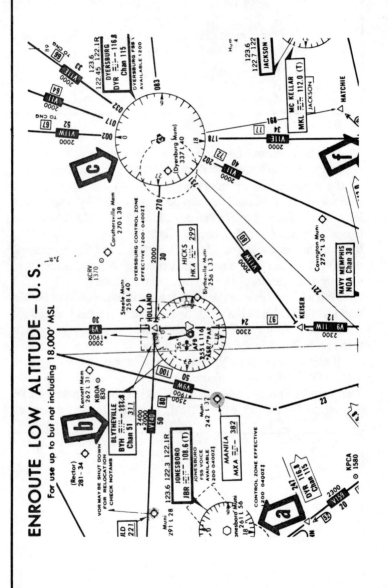

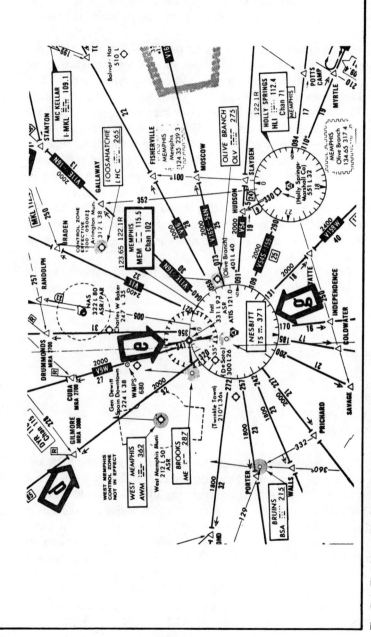

Fig. 5-4. The Memphis area enroute low altitude chart.

is the TO envelope. There are two off sections dividing the envelopes. The handiness of this aid is that one can draw it and place it on a chart during the test or when you are flying for real. Now to explain how it works. Let's use the previous question to illustrate.

In the question, there was only one VOR figure or reference shown. That is the one you must use. First, draw the figure shown (Fig. 5-3). Make it small enough to fit easily over the intersection and not cover the chart very much. About an inch and a-half square will be perfect. The top of the arrow represents the OBS. Place the center of the VOR aid on the Gill VOR. Next, orient the arrow to point the same direction the 248 degree radial does. Now the VOR aid is oriented properly. Referring to the figure in the question, you will see that the radial is to the right with a FROM indication. Going to your homemade VOR aid, check for the corresponding quadrant. Locating it, you will find that you are still south of the intersection and approaching. To find if you are right or left of course, you must go the RMI figure as before in the question explanation.

The VOR aid comes in handy in confusing questions like the following one (refer to Fig. 5-4):

Which combination of indications is proper for beginning the turn at STANTON Intersection (f) while enroute from MEM (g) to DRY (c) on V11E? (See Fig. 5-5).

1. X and Z
2. W and Z
3. W and Y
4. W and X

The easiest way to attack this problem is to use the VOR aid. It will not confuse you. The confusing part of this problem is that there is no FROM indications from any VOR that would make up STANTON Intersection except our on-course radial outbound from MEM VOR.

To orient the VOR aid for this problem, place the crossbars at STANTON Intersection. Because all of the VOR depictions in the problem have an OBS of 358 degrees, the arrow must be oriented to the 358-degree radial also. Therefore, you should now have the crossbars centered at STANTON Intersection and the OBS arrow pointing north towards DRY VOR.

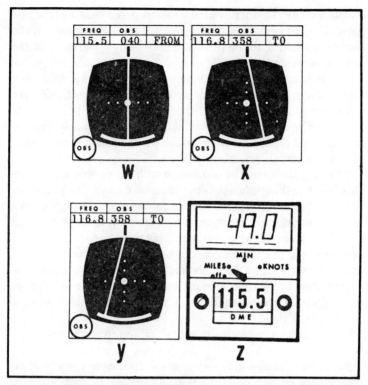

Fig. 5-5. Position the VOR aid, check these, and you can't miss the question.

Because the question asks what the indication to begin the turn will be, you can assume that you are not to STANTON yet. V11E crosses through the TO to the right quadrant of our VOR aid. Thus, the depiction that is correct will be the one with a needle deflection to the right and a TO indication. That figure is labeled "X." The on-course figure is labeled "W." Hence, choice No. 4 is the correct one. Simple. All done with the figure that reads back the correct answer to you. All you need to remember is to draw the VOR aid, and then draw it on the scratch paper the FAA provides for the test.

ADF ORIENTATION

In orienting yourself to an ADF, two instruments must be consulted: the ADF pointer and the directional gyro. The orientation process is very simple. A course is given for you to fly. It could be any of the 360 degrees. For an example, let's use the course of 360 degrees. To orient yourself, 360 degrees must be flown on the directional gyro. Now you can look at the ADF pointer. If the pointer is pointing to the right, the 360- degree bearing is to the right. If it points left, the 360-degree bearing is to the left. If the needle is pointing past the 90- degree mark on either side, then the station is behind us. Again for example, the directional gyro is indicating 360 degrees and the ADF pointer is pointing 170 degrees. The course is to our right, and the station is behind us. Basically, for testing purposes on the written exam, these are the only fundamentals you need to know.

You can, however, be one course with the directional gyro indicating something other than the intended course. The reason for this is a wind correction angle or possibly an interception of a given bearing just prior to turning on course. If you were crabbing to the right 15 degrees, for wind correction, but were on course, the ADF pointer would point 15 degrees to one side also. The side would depend on whether we were inbound or outbound from the beacon. A correction to the right inbound would deflect the needle to the left of north. A correction to the right outbound would deflect the needle to the right.

Another representative question for you from the test:

What is your position with respect to the 190-degree course and the beacon while making an NDB RWY 19 approach? (Refer to Fig. 5-6.)

1. You are right of course and inbound to the beacon.
2. You are on course and outbound from the beacon.
3. You are on course and past the beacon inbound.
4. You are left of course and past the beacon inbound.

The correct choice is No. 4. The directional gyro in this problem indicates a heading of 195 degrees. This could be the final ap-

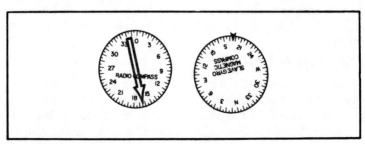

Fig. 5-6. Question reference material.

proach course, a wind correction, or a course correction. It doesn't matter. The ADF pointer is 15 degrees to the right of the tail (180-degree relative bearing if you'd rather call it that). With the needle to the right of the tail, you can deduce that you are left of course and past the beacon inbound to the runway.

DME

One of the handiest things in the cockpit since the thermos jug is Distance Measuring Equipment (DME). See Fig. 5-7. Today's equipment will measure your distance from the station in nautical miles, figure ground speed in knots, and tell you the time it will take to fly to the station at that ground speed. Unfortunately, there is one inherent error in the system. Because an aircraft flies at some distance above the ground, the absolute distance to VOR or TACAN is never known. The distance that the DME measures is actually the hypotenuse of a triangle. It is because of this that when an aircraft flies over a VORTAC at 5,000 feet above the ground, the DME will register one mile to the station. Thus, the greatest error is at high altitudes close to the station.

How can station passage of a VORTAC be determined by use of the DME?

1. The range indicator will decrease until indicating the height above the station, then it will start increasing.
2. The range indicator will read zero upon station passage.
3. The range indicator will stop decreasing the 1/4 mile from the station, and at 1/4 mile past the station, will start increasing.
4. The range indicator will unlock when 1/4 mile from the station and will "search" until 1/4 mile past the station, when it will lock on.

The answer is clearly No. 1. The range will decrease until the height above the station in *miles* is registered, then it will begin to increase. Other questions on DME will pertain to the greatest error in DME which was just discussed, as well as what functions can a DME display.

RADIO ORIENTATION ON THE APPROACH

Knowing when to turn and intercept the final approach course that will take you to the runway is to know how to execute one

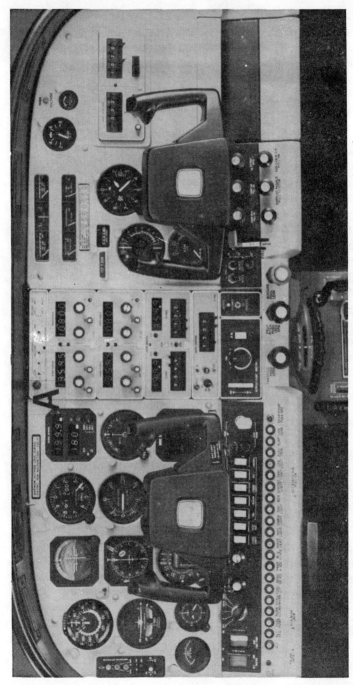

Fig. 5-7. Note the DME at "A." The top number is nautical miles to go. The bottom number is ground speed.

of the finer points to instrument flying. A good instrument pilot doesn't stroll up to the localizer and then turn when the needle centers. That would throw your passengers around and high angles of bank would be necessary.

The DME arc is actually not used greatly, because there are so many radar installations. The DME arc is structured, though, to provide a radial off the VORTAC and provide just the proper amount of lead to start a turn to a localizer or VORTAC approach. This technique is the subject of the next FAA test question. Notice that there are two lead-in radials. Read the markings on the approach plate carefully and the correct lead-in will be apparent. See Fig. 5-8.

Which indications show that you should turn from the 12 DME Arc to the final approach course on the LOC? (See Fig. 5-9.)

1. L and N.
2. M and N.
3. L and O.
4. M and O.

The correct choice is No. 3. This choice shows the 300 degrees radial center. There are two lead-in radials. The 323- and the 300-degree. The only one represented in the question is the 300-degree radial; therefore, it is the correct one. Choosing which localizer depiction is correct is a little harder. The thing to remember is that the front course of a localizer is the same as following a VOR radial. A back course as reverse sensing, thus, you must fly away from the needle to center it. The best way I have found to remember this is to say to myself when examining a back course of even flying one that "the needle is the airplane." Let me say that again, "The needle is the airplane." In this example, you are following the 12 DME arc to the southwest of the airport. If you face the runway for the approach, the localizer is on your left. The aircraft must be to the right. If "the needle is the airplane," then you must also look for the needle to the right. Therefore, figure "0" is the correct one. Using "L" and "O" you will find answer No. 3 to be correct.

A brief look at glide slope orientation. The glide slope is easy to understand. One simply follows the needle. If the needle is low, then you must descend to reach the glide path. If the needle is above

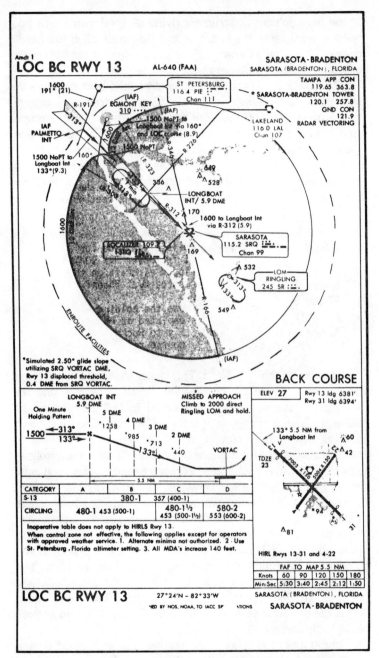

Fig. 5-8. Follow the DME arc on both sides to the lead-in radial. Compare the radials to the localizer and VOR indications to obtain the correct answer.

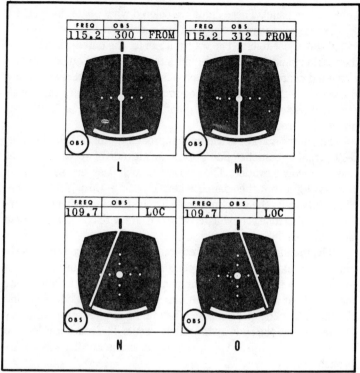

FREQ	OBS	
115.2	300	FROM

L

FREQ	OBS	
115.2	312	FROM

M

FREQ	OBS	
109.7		LOC

N

FREQ	OBS	
109.7		LOC

O

Fig. 5-9. Question reference.

the donut, then you are low and must adjust to fly up. Simply it is—needle up—fly up.

What is your position relative to the Glide Slope and LOC? (See Fig. 5-10.)

1. Low and to the left.
2. Low and to the right.
3. High and to the right.
4. High and to the left.

Occasionally, the FAA will slip the unusual combination of back course localizer with a glide slope. Be sure you RTFQ. In this question, however, it is simply an ILS, and answer No. 3 is correct.

ILS MARKER BEACONS

Generally on instrument-equipped airplanes, there are three

lights on the panel. Those lights are colored white, blue, and yellow. Also, these receivers are capable of emitting an aural tone as well as lighting those lights. The transmitters for the outer marker, middle marker, and fan and bone markers are located on or near the extended centerlines of the approach. The transmitters are of low power—only three watts—and operate at 75 MHz. They radiate an elliptical pattern 2400 feet long and 4200 feet wide at 1,000 feet above the ground.

The outer marker is the final approach fix for a ILS. (See Fig. 5-11.) It intersects the glide slope at an altitude of about 1,400 feet above runway elevation. The transmitter will flash the blue marker beacon light on the panel when crossing through its area. Simultaneously, the synchronized with the flashing, will be an audible tone. This tone is modulated at 400 Hertz with continuous Morse Code dashes.

The middle marker is located 3500-feet from the runway threshold on the extended runway centerline. The transmitter will illuminate the amber light on the panel and will have an aural tone modulated at 1300 Hertz with alternating Morse Code dots and dashes. The glide slope crosses the middle marker approximately 200 feet above the runway touchdown zone. The marker is located just prior to the missed approach point and is not the missed approach point proper.

The white light on the flight panel is reserved for both the back course and inner marker where one is installed. An inner marker is placed at the runway threshold and is used for Category II approaches at large airports. The inner marker is very high- pitched and is transmitted in a series of dots.

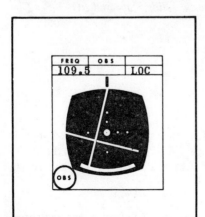

Fig. 5-10. Question reference.

Fig. 5-11. Notice the marker beacons at "A." They are labeled from bottom to top, Outer (O), Middle (M), and Inner (I).

Which code signal should you observe on the marker beacon lights as you pass over the OM on an ILS approach?

1. Alternate dots and dashes.
2. Code for OM (- - -,- - -).
3. A series of dots.
4. A series of dashes.

Answer No. 4 is correct. Remember it this way. The outer marker is dashed. The middle combines dots and dashes and the inner is dotted. From the outer marker towards the runway the codes become progressively more dotted. Got it?

Another navigation aid on an ILS approach is the compass locator. The compass locator is a nondirectional beacon, but an ILS does not have to contain a compass locator to be complete. The compass locator is usually collocated with the outer marker. It has a coded identifier that only has two letters. For example, if the airports' identifier was OKC, the compass locator identifier would be the first two letters, OK.

Try this question:

What would be the compass locator identifier for SPS?

1. PS
2. IPS
3. ISPS
4. SP

Choice No. 4 is correct. Another question the FAA would ask is on the two-letter identifier as compared with marker beacons. Just remember marker beacons have no identifiers. Compass locators have two-letter identifier.

Prudent question reading will save lots of time and mistakes. The main curves the FAA throws on radio orientation is trying to confuse the applicant with other areas. For instance, they will show you a picture of a glide slope and localizer needle. If the question happens to mention that the localizer is a back course, haste may cause you to miss the question. Also, they throw marker beacons and compass locators into the same bag, and they do not go together. Once again, the task is to sort through the extraneous information and get to the target question. If a question confuses you, throw out the part that confuses you and see if it makes any more sense at that point.

HOLDING PATTERN ENTRIES OR
THE PILOT TRAINER DIRECT METHOD

On the new versions of the FAA exam, there are questions about holding pattern entries. These always seem to upset a new instrument pilot student. There should be no reason to miss the exam questions using the following method. Because you have already used the handy-dandy VOR aid, it should be easy for you to adapt to the holding pattern entry aid, which is also handy and dandy.

The Pilot Trainer Direct aid can be drawn in just a second on a scrap piece of paper provided graciously by the FAA (see Fig. 5- 12). Now I realize that the holding patterns are divided by a 70-110 line. This is a mere distraction for any work you have to do either on the test or actual IFR. Therefore, you should draw the Pilot Trainer Direct aid on a regular 90-270 line. To use the aid, just place the crossbars on the intersection or facility with the tail trailing in the direction given in the clearance. For example, if the clearance is to hold north, the tail should point north. This will properly orient the aid for you. Now, simply consult which quadrant you will be in when you arrive, and the aid will give you the proper entry pattern. Pilot stands for parallel, trainer is for teardrop, and direct is obvious.

Try the next question, referring to the same figure as used before (Fig. 4-1).

You have been cleared to hold south of WHEAL Intersection (c) on

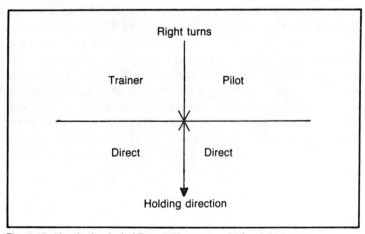

Fig. 5-12. Handy-dandy holding pattern entry aid for right turns.

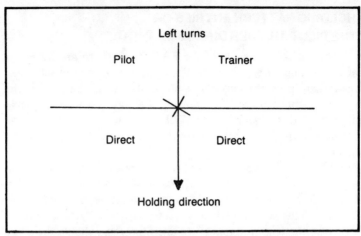

Fig. 5-13. Handy-dandy holding pattern entry aid for left turns.

the Huntsville Localizer, left-hand turns. If you approach WHEAL from DCU VOR on R-131 what type entry is recommended? (No wind correction required.) Use Fig. 5-13.

1. Direct only.
2. Teardrop only.
3. Parallel only.
4. Teardrop or parallel.

The proper holding pattern entry is parallel. Did you get it correct? I'm sure that you did. Incidentally, No. 3 is the proper choice.

Also, I'd like to add that this same method works in the aircraft. If you superimpose this aid over the directional gyro, the holding pattern entries are readily available. All you must do is check which quadrant the holding radial falls into on the present heading. The quadrant it falls into will be the correct holding pattern entry. For example, you are heading 360 degrees. You are assigned to hold on the 131-degree radial southeast. The 131-radial falls in the right-hand lower quadrant, which is assigned the direct entry. Right hand turns, of course. It is all very simple, and little practice with your own charts will go a long way to preparing you for the exam and your instrument flying career.

Chapter 6

Flight Planning and the AIM

You learned while reviewing Part 91 of the FARs that according to 91.5 each pilot in command shall, before beginning a flight, familiarize himself with all available information pertaining to that flight. Much of that information must be extracted from use of the Airman's Information Manual. The purpose of this chapter is to examine flight planning problems and flight planning information found in the AIM.

Part 3 of the AIM contains much information concerning route planning. Among this information is a tabulation of preferred IFR routes. Generally speaking, the questions on the written exam are ones that pertain to reading and interpreting portions of the AIM.

Plan an IFR route from Kennedy International (j) to Boston (d) (Fig. 6-1) which will minimize delays and changes while enroute. Depart 1330Z and cruise 13,000 feet.

1. V229 HFD V292 BOS
2. V229 MAD V475 BOS
3. Belle Terre V229 MAD V475
4. V16 BOS

The correct way to answer this question is to go directly to the AIM excerpt. The mistake the FAA expects one to make is to go to the flight planning chart and try to pick your way through the

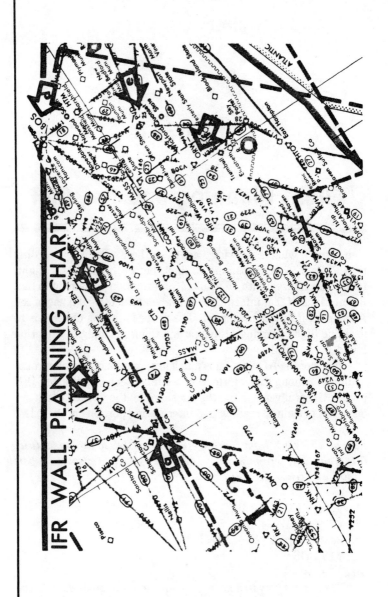

IFR WALL PLANNING CHART

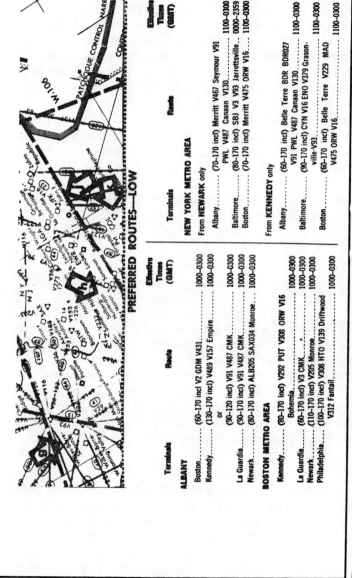

PREFERRED ROUTES—LOW

Terminals	Route	Effective Times (GMT)
ALBANY		
Boston	(60–170 incl) V2 GDM V431	1000–0300
Kennedy	(130–170 incl) V489 V157 Empire	1000–0300
	or	
	(90–120 incl) V91 V487 CMK	1000–0300
La Guardia	(90–170 incl) V91 V487 CMK	1000–0300
Newark	(80–170 incl) ALB205 SAX034 Monroe	1000–0300
BOSTON METRO AREA		
Kennedy	(80–170 incl) V292 PUT V308 ORW V16 Bohemia	1000–0300
La Guardia	(60–170 incl) V3 CMK	1000–0300
Newark	(110–170 incl) V205 Monroe	1000–0300
Philadelphia	(100–170 incl) V308 HTO V139 Driftwood V312 Fantail	1000–0300

Terminals	Route	Effective Times (GMT)
NEW YORK METRO AREA		
From NEWARK only		
Albany	(70–170 incl) Merritt V467 Seymour V91 PWL V487 Canaan V130	1100–0300
Baltimore	(80–170 incl) SB1 V3 V93 Jarrettsville	0000–2359
Boston	(70–170 incl) Merritt V475 ORW V16	1100–0300
From KENNEDY only		
Albany	(60–170 incl) Belle Terre BDR BDR027 V91 PWL V487 Canaan V130	1100–0300
Baltimore	(90–170 incl) CYN V16 ENO V379 Grasonville-V93	1100–0300
Boston	(60–170 incl) Belle Terre V229 MAD V475 ORW V16	1100–0300

Fig. 6-1. Preferred routes are used to expedite and separate arriving traffic from departing traffic.

105

maze of Victor airways. Although one could do that, it probably would come back in a clearance the way you filed it. The purpose of a preferred route is to expedite traffic into and out of airports. Generally, the large airports have separate arterics for arrivals and departures. It is something like the freeway system into and out of large cities. These preferred routes are listed in the computer at an Air Route Traffic Control Center. If you file any other route during peak times of the day, the computer will split a preferred route back at you. At low traffic times, you may get a shorter more direct route that was authorized by a controller overriding the computer. Therefore, from Kennedy to Boston the route should be as written from the peak times of 1100-030 OZ. The correct choice is No. 3.

Lots of answers on AIM questions seem to be obscure if they are there at all. There will be a legend for reference on the test. The FAA does not expect an applicant to remember all symbols and order of printing. One such difficult question is below.

On which frequency can you receive automatic weather broadcasts at Lambert-St. Louis? (See Table 6-1).

1. 111.0 MHz
2. 338 kHz
3. 120.45 MHz
4. 117.4 MHz

The answer does not seem to be readily apparent. Choice No. 2 is correct. That little black box shown in Table 6-1 indicates a transcribed weather broadcast. A trip to the legend in Fig. 6-2 explains the black box, then answer choice becomes simple. If anything is to be learned here, it is to consult the legend. If you try to answer the question from deductive reasoning or memory of the legend, you will probably be wrong. Save those points for more complex questions, you may need them.

NOTAMS

Another area that seems to lack adequate attention in textbooks in the area of FDC NOTAMs. The FAA seems to pay particular attention to these. The initials FDC stand for the National Flight Data Center. FDC NOTAMs differ from regular notices to airmen because they deal with information that is regulatory in nature. For example, FDC NOTAMs are disseminated to amend current

ST. LOUIS FSS 121.5 122.0 122.1R 122.2 122.6

I ST LOUIS, LAMBERT-ST LOUIS INTL (STL) *IFR* 10NW LRA

FSS: ST LOUIS on Fld
589 H100/12R-30L(4) (S-100, D-184, DT-346) BL6,7A,8,11,12,13 S5
F18,34,40 U2 **VASI: Rwy** 30R **RVR-2: Rwy** 24, 12R **REIL:**
Rwy 12L, 30R

Remarks: Rwy 12R thr dsplcd 458'. A-gear all rwys except
12L-30R and 17-35. Arresting Cables rwy 12R 1125' from
threshold, rwy 30L 610' from threshold, rwy 6 1509' from
threshold, rwy 24 622' from threshold. Rwy 6-24 grooved.
Cert.-FAR 139, CFR Index D.

St. Louis Tower 118.5 120.05   **Gnd Con** 121.65 121.9
‡ **Clrnc Del** 119.5
ATIS 120.45 110.3

Radar Services:
St. Louis App Con 126.5 (117-297°) 123.7 125.15 (298-116°)
St. Louis Dep Con 124.9 (117-297°) 119.9 (298-116°)
TCA Group 2 See NOS TCA Chart
ILS 110.3 I-STL **Rwy** 24 **LOM:** 404/ST
ILS 109.7 I-LMR **Rwy** 12R **LOM:** 338■ /LM
.**ILS** 109.7 I-BKY **Rwy** 30L
St. Louis (H) VORTAC 117.4/STL 138° 8.0NM to fld.
NDB H-SAB■ 117° 5.3NM to rwy 12R (see Limestone)
NDB MHW 238° 4.2NM to rwy 24 (see Steeple)

Remarks: Rwy 12R LOM is Limestone NDB■. Rwy 24 LOM is
Steeple NDB. **VOT:** 111.0.

- -

I SPIRIT OF ST LOUIS (SUS) *IFR* 20W FSS: ST LOUIS (LC 532-3513)
462 H60/7-25(1) (S-33, D-50, DT-80) L6,7A S5 F12,18,30
Ox1,2,3,4 U2
Remarks: Based acft only auth touch and go opns.
Spirit Tower 118.3   **Gnd Con** 121.7
Radar Services:
St. Louis App Con 126.5 123.7
St. Louis Dep Con 124.9
Stage I Ctc St. Louis App Con
ILS 111.9 I-SUS **Rwy** 7 **LOM:** 326/SU
Remarks: Twr opers 0600-2200. Rwy 7 BC unusable beyond
15NM.

aeronautical charts, instrument approach procedures, or restrictions
to flight. the FDC NOTAMs are distributed through the National
Communications Center in Kansas City. The important thing to
remember is that FDC NOTAMs are regulatory.

*Why should you review the latest FDC NOTAMs during preflight
planning for an IFR flight?*

1. To find the restrictions to en route navigation aids.
2. To be aware of all of the latest flight safety information.
3. To obtain the latest information on the status of navigation
   facilities.

4. To see if there have been changes made that will affect an approach procedure that you might make.

Answer No. 4 is correct. It is the answer that would pertain to regulatory information, such as changes in aeronautical charts or changes in instrument approach procedures. Choice No. 2 looks good, but the regular NOTAMs cover information pertaining to flight safety also.

The FAA gets down to the foundation of FDC NOTAMs. If one is not familiar with the use of FDC NOTAMs, it is possible to miss questions like the following:

What is the new landing minimum for Category B aircraft on the NDB RWY 18 approach at Le Mars Municipal, Le Mars, Iowa? (See Table 6-2.)

1. Ceiling 1,960 feet and visibility increased by 1/4 mile.
2. Visibility 1/4 mile.
3. Visibility increased by 1/4 mile.
4. Ceiling 1,960 feet and visibility 1/4 mile.

Answer No. 3 is correct. The choice is a difficult one. Choice No. 1 looks correct, but No. 1 says the ceiling must be 1960 feet and the visibility increased by 1/4 mile. The trouble is, visibility is the only minimum to any approach. If the field is reporting a visibility equal to the landing minimum, a pilot may shoot the approach. If the runway or its environment is in sight at the missed approach point, a landing may be made regardless of the ceiling.

Part 3 of AIM also has a tabulation of restrictions to enroute navigation aids. The listing is arranged in alphabetical order of the state in which the facility is located.

What action, if any, should permit an IFR flight to receive accurate navigation signals from the Buckeye VORTAC (Arizona) beyond 28 NM on a magnetic course of 070 degrees from the facility? (See Table 6-3.)

1. Maintain an altitude at or above 4,000 feet.
2. No action, the radial is unusable.
3. Use dual VORs and average the indication.
4. Set 252 degrees on the OBS and use the reverse sensing feature.

Table 6-2. FDC NOTAM.

F.A.A. NATIONAL FLIGHT DATA CENTER

FDC NOTAMS

THE LISTING BELOW INCLUDES, IN PART, CHANGES IN FLIGHT DATA, PARTICULARLY OF A REGULATORY NATURE, THAT AFFECTS STANDARD INSTRUMENT APPROACH PROCEDURES, AERONAUTICAL CHARTS AND SELECTED FLIGHT RESTRICTIONS, PRIOR TO THEIR NORMAL PUBLICATION CYCLE. THEREFORE, THEY SHOULD BE REVIEWED DURING PRE-FLIGHT PLANNING. THIS LISTING INCLUDES ALL FDC NOTAMS CURRENT THRU FDC NOTAM NUMBER SHOWN BELOW. FDC NOTAMS ISSUED FOLLOWING THIS NUMBER ARE AVAILABLE AT ALL F.A.A.FLIGHT SERVICE STATIONS.

LEGEND

FDC ------- NATIONAL FLIGHT DATA CENTER
4/103 ----- ACCOUNTABILITY NUMBER ASSIGNED TO THE MESSAGE ORIGINATOR BY FDC
FI/T ------ FLIGHT INFORMATION/TEMPORARY
FI/P ------ FLIGHT INFORMATION/PERMANENT
● --------- NEW NOTAM

THE FOLLOWING LISTING CONTAINS ALL FDC NOTAMS
THRU FDC 6/313

SOUTHWEST

TEXAS

FDC 5/171 FI/T MILLER INTERNATIONAL MCALLEN TX. LOC/BC RWY 31 ORIG NA.

FDC 6/8 FI/T ROBERT MUELLER MUNI AUSTIN TX. VORTAC RWY 12R AMDT 3 SI ALL CAT MDA 1100FT HAT 470FT CRCG CAT C MDA 1160FT HAA 528FT. VORTAC RWY 16R AMDT 2 ILS RWY 30L AMDT 26 NDB RWY 30L AMDT 26 CRCG CAT C MDA 160FT HAA 528FT.

FDC 6/232 FI/T SAN ANTONIO INTERNATIONAL SAN ANTONIO TX. SI MINS NA FOR NDB RWY 30L /ILS RWY 30L/LOC RWY 30L/RNAV RWY 30L/NDB RWY 12R/ILS RWY 12R/LOC RWY 12R.

WEST CENTRAL

IOWA

FDC 5/885 FI/T BOONE MUNI BOONE IA. NDB RWY 14 AMDT 2 SI MDA 1900FT HAT 753FT ALL CAT. VSBY CAT B 11/4MI CAT C 11/2MI CAT D 13/4MI. CRCG MDA 1900FT HAA 753FT ALL CAT. VSBY CAT B 11/4MI.

FDC 6/158 FI/T LE MARS MUNI LE MARS IA. NDB RWY 18 AMDT 2 SI AND CRCG MDA 1960FT ALL CAT. VSBY CAT B C D AND CRCG CAT B INCR 1/4MI.

FDC 6/159 FI/T WEBSTER CITY MUNI WEBSTER CITY IA. NDB RWY 32 AMDT 2 SI MDA 1680FT ALL CAT. CRCG MDA 1680FT CAT A B C.

109

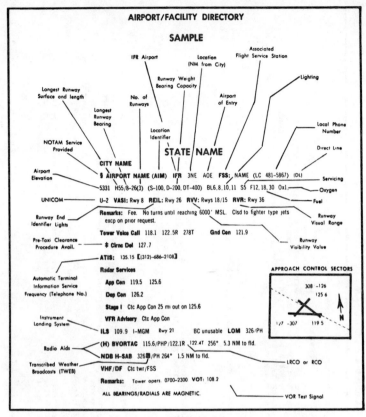

Fig. 6-2. The legend for Part 3 of the Airman's Information Manual.

This question is directly from the written exam. Choice No. 1 is correct. On a magnetic course of 060-075 degrees an altitude above 4,000 feet must be maintained to maintain reception of the Buckeye VORTAC.

FLIGHT PLANNING (FUEL ESTIMATES AND AIRCRAFT PERFORMANCE)

The Test questions on computer operations are a great deal easier than they previously were. In years past, before the new format of written exam, there was a flight log that had to be filled out. Many times, this log could not be completed if an applicant was unable to fill even one blank. Today, the FAA is a little more fair. For instance, fuel problems don't depend on information derived from performance tables.

Radio Facility Restrictions are cited until cancelled by the Associated Station.

Restricted areas are defined in degrees from magnetic North.

ALABAMA

BROOKLEY VORTAC: VOR portion unusable beyond 30 mi below 2,000 MSL.

EUFAULA VORTAC: DME portion unusable beyond 35 NM, below 1900' MSL beyond 35 NM, below 2400' MSL beyond 40 NM.

GADSDEN VORTAC: VOR portion unusable below 5000' MSL; 237–245° and 309–339° all sectors and altitudes.

MOBILE VORTAC: VOR portion unusable 023–033°.

ARIZONA

BUCKEYE VORTAC: Unusable beyond 28 nmi below 4000' MSL, 000–075°, beyond 35 nmi below 5000' MSL, 230–260°, beyond 35 nmi below 7000' 280–320°, beyond 37 nmi below 6000' MSL 320–360°.

COCHISE VORTAC: Unusable beyond 35 NM below 10,000' MSL, 005–015°, beyond 25 NM below 10,000' MSL, 015–030°, beyond 35 NM below 10,000' MSL, 030–040°, beyond 30 NM below 9,000' MSL 190–220°, beyond 25 NM below 9,200' MSL 220–240°.

DOUGLAS VORTAC: DME portion unusable beyond 26 NM below 10,000' MSL 045–065°; beyond 28 NM below 9500' MSL 065–085°; beyond 35 NM below 11,300' MSL 355–010°.

FLAGSTAFF VOR: Unusable beyond 30 nmi below 8300' MSL, 030–110°, beyond 35 nmi below 10,200' MSL 110–155°; beyond 30 nmi below 9300' MSL 155–245°; beyond 30 nmi below 11,900' MSL, 245–325°; beyond 15 nmi below 14,100' MSL 325–030°.

GRAND CANYON VOR: Unusable 340–030° beyond-30 NM below 10,800' MSL, 030–060° beyond 25 NM below 9600' MSL, 060–100° beyond 20 NM below 9000' MSL, 230–270° beyond 15 NM below 10,000 MSL.

KINGMAN VOR: Unusable beyond 25 NM below 9,000' MSL, 085–130°, beyond 15 NM below 10,000' MSL, 130–180°, beyond 30 NM below 7,000' MSL 180–255°; beyond 35 NM below 9,000' MSL, 255–315°, beyond 20 NM below 8,000' MSL 315–085°.

9100' MSL 185–195° beyond 13 nmi below 9100' MSL 195–220° beyond 25 nmi below 9100' MSL 220–235° beyond 30 nmi below 8900' MSL 265–275°.

SAN SIMON VORTAC: Unusable beyond 30 nmi below 8000' MSL 350–360°, beyond 30 nmi below 8000' MSL 020–050° beyond 28 nmi below 11,300' MSL 150–190°, beyond 30 nmi below 9000' MSL 190–220°, beyond 30 nmi below 9300' MSL 235–250°.

TUCSON VORTAC: Unusable beyond 23 NM below 10,200' MSL 040–095° and beyond 32 NM below 10,700' MSL 325–020°.

YUMA VORTAC: Unusable beyond 27 nmi below 3800' MSL 280–300°.

ARKANSAS

HOT SPRINGS VOR: Unusable 346–055° beyond 20 NM below 3500' MSL.; 056°–140° beyond 20 NM below 6500' MSL; 141–227° beyond 20 NM below 3500' MSL.; 141–227° beyond 28 NM below 5500' MSL; 228–311° beyond 20 NM below 3500' MSL; 312–345° beyond 15 NM below 5500' MSL.; 312–345° beyond 32 NM below 9600' MSL.

PINE BLUFF VORTAC: VOR portion unusable 054–079° beyond 35 NM below 5000' MSL, 170–185° beyond 20 NM below 2000' MSL, 236–249° beyond 20 NM below 6000' MSL or beyond 26 NM below 8000' MSL.

CALIFORNIA

ARCATA VOR: Unusable 090–150° beyond 20 NM below 6000'.

AVENAL VORTAC: DME portion unusable beyond 40 nmi below 3000' MSL 320–065° below 4000' MSL, 065–085° below 4500' MSL, 086–125° below 8500' MSL, 125–170° below 7500' MSL, 170–198° below 7000' MSL, 195–230° below 8000' MSL, 230–305°.

BIG SUR VORTAC: VOR portion unusable 215–235° beyond 16 nmi below 10,000' MSL. DME portion unusable beyond 35 nmi below 9000' MSL 320–085°.

111

Table 6-3. Restrictions to Enroute Navigation Aids from Part 3 of the Airman's Information Manual.

The FAA dwells mostly upon questions that pertain to fuel estimates. The scope of this chapter is not to instruct in the use of flight computers, but to use "the plan of attack" that will make the answers easy to attain.

In Chapter 2, I detailed a plan of attack. Remember "See the target clearly," etc? This plan of attack works on flight planning problems as well. In flight planning problems, however, on the nature of fuel required, you will need a different checklist.

Drawing up a formula sheet will outline the checklist. It will be necessary for you to draw out this checklist for yourself several times in order to remember it. In the last chapter there will be an entire formula sheet to memorize and Fig. 6-3 will be a portion of it:

That is the complete checklist for a fuel required problem. Now, let's use this plan of attack on a sample question from the FAA Instrument Written Exam.

For planning purposes, approximately what minimum fuel is required for an IFR flight from Gardner Muni (c) to Wilkes-Barre—Scranton

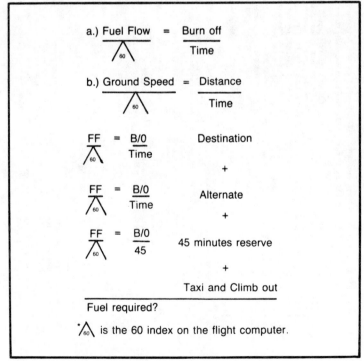

Fig. 6-3. An equation for the fuel required checklist.

Airport (g)? An alternate is required. (Refer back to Fig. 6-1.)

TAS . . . . 177 knots

Wind . . . . Average 20 knots headwind

Route . . . . GDM V106 AVP

Alternate . . . . V106 PWL (Wind 20 knots tailwind)

Fuel Consumption . . . . 13.6 GPH

Add 5.6 gallons for taxi, takeoff, climbout, and landing approach.

1. 29.2 gallons
2. 34.4 gallons
3. 38.8 gallons
4. 42.4 gallons

To begin examination and solving this problem you must first:

1) **See the target clearly.** The target question is, what is the minimum fuel required for an IFR flight?
2) **Plan a checklist.** What do you need to know to solve this problem? To begin with, a great many things. That is where the memorized formula sheet comes into play. Your photographic memory will produce it on command. After spilling it out on paper as it was just done, you will notice that there are two formulas at the top of the formula sheet. They are labeled "a & b" in order of your need of them, which also corresponds to your plan of attack letters a & b

   a) **Is it given?**
   b) **Directly from knowing.**

Now, let's get started picking this one apart. Going to the checklist you see Destination. a.) Is the fuel required to the destination given? No, it is not. b) Can you find it directly from knowing other factors? Yes, you can. Going to the formula "b" you need to know the ground speed and the distance to find the amount of time you will be burning fuel.

To find the distance you must refer to the IFR Wall Planning Chart. The route is listed as GDM V106 AVP. Adding all of the numbers inside the ovals along V106, you find a sum of 185 nautical miles.

Is the ground speed given? No. Can you find it directly from knowing? Yes. If you know the wind and the True Airspeed (TAS), you can figure the ground speed. The TAS is given as 177 knots and the wind is a headwind of 20 knots. Hence, the average ground speed is 157 knots.

Now, you must solve for the time to the destination according to formula "b."

$$\frac{157 \text{ Knots}}{\overset{\wedge}{60}} = \frac{185}{\text{time}}$$

71 minutes = time to destination

Going back to the checklist, you next see the word "alternate."
a.) Is the fuel required to go to the alternate given? No. it is not.
b.) Can you find it directly from knowing something? Yes, if you know all of the factors in the formula *a* you can answer this question. But once again, all of the blanks in formula *a* are not given. Thus, you must find them directly from knowing formula *b*.

Formula *b*. In order to solve for the time, you must have the ground speed enroute to the alternate as well as the distance. Neither are given. So, they must be derived from knowing other information. Once again, the distance to the alternate is found by summing all of the numbers in the oval boxes along the described route V106 PWL. These add up to 102 nautical miles.

The ground speed to the alternate is given as a 20 knot tailwind. Thus, adding 20 knots to your TAS of 177 knots, you arrive at a 197 knot ground speed.

You now have all of the information to solve formula *b*.

$$\frac{197 \text{ knots}}{\overset{\wedge}{60}} = \frac{102 \text{ miles}}{\text{time}}$$

31 minutes = time to alternate

Continuing down the checklist on the formula sheet you will come to the 45-minute reserve. To solve formula *a*, you have the time enroute. This time it is given, 45 minutes. And finally, the fuel required for taxi, takeoff, climbout, and landing is given as 5.6 gallons.

The conclusion of the problem is to now go to the checklist and complete the computations of each formula *a* to the left of the destination, alternate, and 45-minute reserve.

The completed checklist should look like Fig. 6-4.

My computations with an E6-B^2 computer came to 38.9 gals. Choice No. 3 is closest and correct. The error here is one of dif-

$$\frac{13.6 \text{ gph}}{\overset{\triangle}{}_{60}} = \frac{B/0}{71 \text{ min.}} = 16.1 \text{ gals} \quad \text{Destination}$$

$$\frac{13.6 \text{ gph}}{\overset{\triangle}{}_{60}} = \frac{B/0}{31 \text{ min.}} = 7.0 \text{ gals} \quad \underset{\text{Alternate}}{+}$$

$$\frac{13.6 \text{ gph}}{\overset{\triangle}{}_{60}} = \frac{B/0}{45 \text{ min.}} = 10.2 \text{ gals,} \quad \underset{}{+}$$

45 minute Reserve

+

5.6 gals Ground

Fuel Required?   38.9 gals

Fig. 6-4. Plugging numbers into the equation solves the fuel-required problem.

ferences. Remember, the FAA checks each problem with different types of computers. It is unknown which type gave the answer. The answer is sufficiently close to leave no doubt that you have arrived at the correct conclusion, however. Answer No. 1 is a value neglecting the provision for a 45-minute reserve after reaching the alternate. As always, the FAA is ready for your mistakes.

Now, I must apologize for running you through the last problem. This is the second edition of this book, and many things have changed. For example, fuel planning problems. The previous explanation is the way it *was* required, and the formulas are the only method that will work for you in actual flight planning whenever you receive your instrument rating; therefore, I left it for you from the previous edition of the book.

Now, on the new version of the test, only knowledge of how to use a graph is necessary. I will explain this method next, but first I must lash out at the FAA for this type of testing. Plain and simple, a person may learn to read graphs, but nothing may be learned or retained about actual fuel planning. This leaves the new instrument pilot wide open to have a gap in his knowledge. In fact, he may take off someday short of fuel because of insufficient knowledge to plan fuel required correctly. Don't let that be *you*!

The information you need is supplied for the next question in Table 6-4 and Fig. 6-5. Here's the question.

Table 6-4. Operating Conditions and Time, Fuel, Distance to Climb Chart.

OPERATING CONDITIONS		L-1	L-2	L-3	L-4	L-5	L-6
Weight (lb.)		5,500	5,100	4,700	4,900	5,300	5,500
Departure Airport	Pressure Altitude (ft.)	2,000	3,000	S/L	6,000	1,000	S/L
	OAT	20°F	10°C	89°F	60°F	40°F	80°F
Cruise	Pressure Altitude (ft.)	8,500	11,000	12,500	14,000	11,500	6,000
	OAT	ISA	0°C	ISA+10°C	ISA -7°C	32°F	59°F

TIME, FUEL, AND DISTANCE TO CLIMB - MAXIMUM CLIMB

OPERATING CONDITIONS		M-1	M-2	M-3	M-4	M-5	M-6
Weight (lb.)		5,500	5,300	5,100	4,900	4,700	5,500
Departure Airport	Pressure Altitude (ft.)	1,000	1,500	2,000	3,000	4,000	5,000
	OAT	95°F	80°F	60°F	90°F	32°F	50°F
Cruise	Pressure Altitude (ft.)	9,000	10,500	8,000	9,000	12,000	14,000
	OAT	50°F	ISA	ISA+11°C	40°C	ISA+10°C	ISA

TIME, FUEL AND DISTANCE TO CLIMB - MAXIMUM CLIMB

NOTE: 1. Time, fuel and distance for the climb are determined by taking the difference between the departure airport and cruise altitude conditions.

2. For total fuel used, add 25 pounds for start, taxi and takeoff.

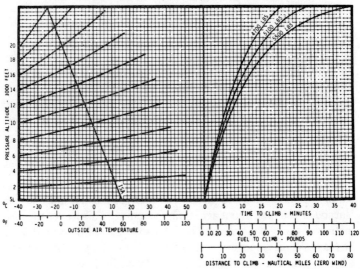

Fig. 6-5. Charting the time, fuel, distance equation to maximum climb.

What is the time, fuel, and distance for operating conditions L-1? (See Table 6-4 and Fig. 6-5.)

1. Eight min., 34 lb., and 14 NM.
2. Seven min., 29 lb., and 12 NM.
3. Six min., 24 lb., and 10 NM.
4. Five min., 21 lb., and 8 NM.

Here's how to arrive at the proper answer. First, you are going from a field elevation of the departure airport given as a pressure altitude of 2,000 feet. You must climb to a cruise altitude of 8,500 feet or a difference of 6,500 feet. Therefore, you enter the graph of Fig. 6-5 at the 6,500-foot pressure altitude. Then you parallel the 6,000-foot line below to the temperature of 20° F. Be certain to use the Fahrenheit line and not the Celsius line. Once reaching the 20° F. line, read horizontally across the page to the 5,500-pound line. Incidentally, a straightedge will increase your accuracy. From the 5,500-lb. line, read down to five (5) minutes. Directly below will be the fuel to climb and distance to climb, which will read 21 lbs. and 8 mi. respectively.

Try the next two questions for practice.

What is the time, fuel, and distance for operating conditions L-3? Use Table 6-4 and Fig. 6-5.

1. Eight min., 30 lb., and 12 NM.
2. Nine min., 38 lb., and 18 NM.
3. Eleven min., 48 lb., and 21 NM.
4. Twelve min., 51 lb., and 22 NM.

Answer No. 3 is correct.

What is the time, fuel, and distance for operating conditions L-4?

1. Six min., 21 lb., and 12 NM.
2. Seven., 26 lb., and 14 NM.
3. Eight min., 27 lb., and 15 NM.
4. Ten min., 40 lb., and 19 NM.

Choice No. 1 is correct.

TAKEOFF AND LANDING

As prescribed by 91.5 of the FARs, a pilot needs to know the takeoff and landing distance of his aircraft into unfamiliar airports. I will discuss these, neglecting climb and cruise performance, because computing climb and cruise by charge is essentially the same.

Nine times out of ten the FAA questions involve interpolation. The problem on calculating takeoff distance is an example.

What is the approximate takeoff distance over a 50-foot obstacle if the temperature is standard at 3,500 feet, the airplane weight is 3,800 lbs., and the wind is calm? (See Table 6-5.)

1. 2,296 feet
2. 2.224 feet
3. 2,382 feet
4. 2,339 feet

To begin the problem, it is first important to find the proper columns to use. The gross weight is 3,800 lbs. That will be the top category across the chart. Also, the wind is described in the question as being calm. So you use the appropriate numbers in the 3800-lb. column.

The plan of attack will work well with this problem, but there is an additional formula that can help simplify the thought process and minimize mistakes.

Table 6-5. Takeoff Data Chart.

TAKE-OFF DISTANCE WITH 10° FLAPS FROM HARD SURFACE RUNWAY										
			@ SEA LEVEL & 59° F.		@ 2500 FT. & 50°F.		@ 5000 FT. & 41°F		@ 7500 FT. & 32°F	
GROSS WEIGHT POUNDS	IAS @ 50 FT.	HEAD WIND KNOTS	GROUND RUN	TOTAL TO CLEAR 50 FT. OBS.	GROUND RUN	TOTAL TO CLEAR 50 FT. OBS.	GROUND RUN	TOTAL TO CLEAR 50 FT. OBS.	GROUND RUN	TOTAL TO CLEAR 50 FT. OBS.
3800	82	0	1170	2030	1305	2210	1465	2425	1645	2665
		10	870	1610	985	1765	1115	1950	1270	2155
		20	615	1225	705	1360	810	1515	935	1695
3400	77	0	905	1605	1010	1745	1135	1905	1275	2085
		10	660	1255	745	1375	850	1510	965	1670
		20	455	945	520	1040	600	1160	695	1290
3000	72	0	680	1270	760	1375	850	1495	960	1635
		10	485	985	550	1070	625	1175	715	1290
		20	325	725	370	795	430	885	500	980

NOTES: 1. Increase distance 10% for each 20°F above standard temperature for particular altitude.
2. For operation on a dry, grass runway, increase distances (both "ground run" and "total to clear 50 ft. obstacle") by 5% of the "total to clear 50 ft. obstacle" figure.

$$\frac{\text{Chart Altitude Change}}{\text{Chart Change in distance}} = \frac{\text{Your Altitude Change}}{\text{Your Distance Change}}$$

In this formula the important thing to remember is that the word "change" means difference or subtract. Step by step let's complete the formula.

First, the chart altitude change is the difference between the 5,000 feet altitude 2,500-foot altitude level. You use these two columns from the chart because your problem altitude is 3,500 feet, which is somewhere between 2,500 feet and 5,000 feet. Thus, the chart altitude change is 2,500 feet.

Next, you find the difference in distance on the chart between 2,425 feet at 5,000 feet and 2210 feet at 2,500 feet. The difference is 215 feet. That completes the chart side of the formula.

The problem side or answer side of the formula must now be completed. The altitude change in the problem is 1,000 feet. This is the difference of 3,500-foot level in the question and the lowest chart column that is being referred to, which is 2,500 feet. The change in takeoff distance is what you need to solve for in this problem in order to arrive at an adjusted takeoff distance over a 50-foot obstacle. Hence, your formula should look like this:

$$\frac{2500}{215} = \frac{1000}{X}$$

$$2500X = 215,000$$

$$X = 86 \text{ feet}$$

Now, you have found the change in takeoff distance with a 1,000-foot increase in altitude. To arrive at the proper answer, now add:

2210 feet (from the 2500-foot level)
+ 86 feet
2296 feet

Answer No. 1 is the correct choice. This method of interpolation can be used on all charts of this type. The important thing is to use the "plan of attack," which will lead you step-by-step in the proper thought process. The formula just discussed will be presented in the formula memory sheet at the end of the book.

Determining landing distance is essentially the same as take-

Table 6-6. Landing Distance.

		LANDING DISTANCE WITH 30° FLAPS ON HARD SURFACED RUNWAY							
GROSS WEIGHT POUNDS	APPROACH IAS MPH	@ SEA LEVEL & 59°F		@ 2500 FEET & 50°F		@ 5000 FEET & 41°F		@ 7500 FEET & 32°F	
		GROUND ROLL	TOTAL TO CLEAR 50 FT. OBS.	GROUND ROLL	TOTAL TO CLEAR 50 FT. OBS.	GROUND ROLL	TOTAL TO CLEAR 50 FT. OBS.	GROUND ROLL	TOTAL TO CLEAR 50 FT. OBS.
3800	82	765	1500	815	1595	865	1695	920	1805

NOTES: 1. Distances shown are based on zero wind, power off, and heavy braking.

2. Reduce ground roll 10% for each 5 knots headwind. For total landing distance, reduce "total to clear 50 ft obstacle figure by 10% for each 5 knots headwind.

off distance. Using the interpolation formula and the "plan of attack" will work on this question.

What is the landing distance over a 50-foot obstacle under standard conditions at 1,000 feet with a 15-knot headwind? (See Table 6-6.)

1. 1,791 feet.
2. 1,090 feet.
3. 1,557 feet.
4. 1,323 feet.

$$\frac{\text{CHART Alt. Change}}{\text{Chart Change in distance}} = \frac{\text{Your Alt. Change}}{\text{Your Distance Change}}$$

Once again, the chart altitude change is 2,500 feet. This is because our given altitude in the problem is 1,500 feet and this falls between sea level and 2,500 feet on the chart twenty-five hundred feet minus sea level equals 2,500 feet.

The distance to clear a 50-foot obstacle at 2,500 feet field elevation is 1,595 feet. At sea level that value, according to the chart, is reduced to 1,500 feet. The difference is 95 feet.

The given field elevation in the problem is 1,500 feet. Therefore, the given altitude change from sea level is 1,500 feet. The completed formula appears below:

$$\frac{2500}{95} = \frac{1500}{\text{Your Distance Change}}$$

$$57 = \text{Your Distance Change}$$

Using the logic that at higher field elevations takeoff and landing distances increase, you must add 57 feet to the 1,500-foot sea level figure. The distance to clear the 50-foot obstacle is now 1,557 feet. But wait a minute! You had a 15-knot headwind didn't you. You did, and now we must read the fine print at the bottom of the landing distance table.

The fine print instructs you to decrease the landing distance 10 percent for every 5 knots of headwind. Because you have 15 knots of headwind, your landing distance may be reduced by 30 percent. The easiest way to do this is to subtract 30 percent from 100 percent and multiply the 1,557 feet by 70 percent. Your product is 1089.9 feet, which is very close to answer No. 2, 1,090 feet.

Although in the examples just discussed you did not use the "plan of attack" as such, it should be used. It is important to understand that the "plan of attack" is a form to lead one through the process of deductive reasoning. When using the "plan of attack," it becomes easy to dig out the parts of the question that need to be answered first, then work towards a final solution.

When working with the Airman's Information Manual on the test, the greatest help will come from being familiar with its different parts and its general use. This will save you a great deal of time as well as energy in trying to decipher it at test time. Of course, you can't memorize all of the symbols and the order in which they are laid out. It is important, however, that you recognize the fact that a symbol does indicate something and consult the proper legend.

The process that you just learned still applies to the new testing methods, but the charts have been changed. The important thing to remember when attempting the question below is that Table 6-7 requires that you use the proper section on gross weight, and you should also be aware of the interpolation between temperatures. Finally, take note and adjust your answer for headwinds and tailwinds as prescribed at the top of Table 6-8. You may have to refer additionally to 6-6, the Crosswind Component Chart.

What is the normal takeoff distance for operating conditions D-1? (Use Tables 6-7 and 6-8.)

1. 1,980 ft.
2. 2,205 ft.
3. 2,278 ft.
4. 2,695 ft.

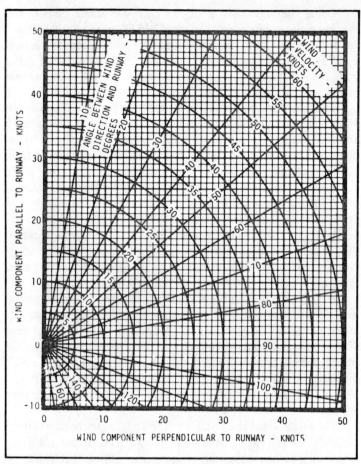

Fig. 6-6. You can determine how wind speed and direction affect takeoff using this chart.

Table 6-7. Normal Takeoff Distance and Operating Conditions.

	NORMAL TAKEOFF DISTANCE					
OPERATING CONDITIONS	D-1	D-2	D-3	D-4	D-5	D-6
Weight (lb.)	5,500	5,300	4,900	4,500	4,300	5,100
Runway	36	18	3	27R	30	26
Runway Surface Level, Hard/Firm, Dry	Concrete	Asphalt	Sod	Sod	Concrete	Asphalt
Wind Direction/Speed	055°/18	280°/10	120°/20	010°/10	015°/20	360°/10
Temperature	23°F	50°F	10°C	41°F	-10°C	5°F
Pressure Altitude (ft.)	3,000	1,500	6,000	1,000	8,500	6,000

To solve this question, use the gross weight of 5500 lbs. on Table 6-8. The temperature is 23°F., which is midway between the 14- and 32-degree values on the chart. At 3,000 feet, one pressure altitude value is 2360 and the other is 2540. These can be found under the 50-foot obstacle column. Averaging these two, you get 2450 feet. Referring to Fig. 6-6 and the crosswind compo-

Table 6-8. Normal Takeoff Distances.

CONDITIONS:
1. Power - FULL THROTTLE and 2700 RPM Before Brake Release
2. Mixtures - LEAN For Field Elevation
3. Wing Flaps - UP
4. Cowl Flaps - OPEN
5. Level, Hard Surface, Dry Runway

NOTE:
1. If full power is applied without brakes set, distances apply from point where full power is applied.
2. Decrease all distances 7° for each 10 knots headwind.
3. Increase all distances 5' for each 2 knots tailwind.
4. Increase all distances 7.9° for operation on firm dry sod runway.

WEIGHT-POUNDS	TAKEOFF TO 50-FOOT OBSTACLE SPEED-KIAS	PRESSURE ALTITUDE-FEET	-20°C (-4°F) GROUND ROLL - FEET	-20°C (-4°F) TOTAL DISTANCE TO CLEAR 50 FEET	-10°C (14°F) GROUND ROLL - FEET	-10°C (14°F) TOTAL DISTANCE TO CLEAR 50 FEET	0°C (32°F) GROUND ROLL - FEET	0°C (32°F) TOTAL DISTANCE TO CLEAR 50 FEET	10°C (50°F) GROUND ROLL - FEET	10°C (50°F) TOTAL DISTANCE TO CLEAR 50 FEET
5500	92	Sea Level	1330	1650	1440	1760	1550	1890	1660	2020
		1000	1470	1810	1580	1940	1700	2080	1830	2240
		2000	1610	1990	1740	2140	1880	2300	2020	2470
		3000	1780	2200	1920	2360	2070	2540	2300	2800
		4000	1970	2430	2130	2620	2370	2900	2550	3120
		5000	2180	2700	2430	2980	2620	3220	2820	3470
		6000	2490	3080	2690	3320	2900	3590	3130	3880
		7000	2770	3440	2990	3730	3240	4040	3500	4380
		8000	3090	3880	3350	4220	3620	4590	3920	5000
		9000	3470	4420	3760	4930	4080	5290	4420	5800
		10,000	3880	5050	4220	5550	4580	6130	4980	6810
5100	88	Sea Level	1110	1380	1200	1480	1290	1580	1380	1690
		1000	1220	1510	1320	1620	1420	1740	1520	1860
		2000	1340	1660	1450	1780	1560	1910	1680	2040
		3000	1480	1820	1600	1960	1720	2100	1850	2250
		4000	1630	2010	1760	2160	1900	2330	2050	2500
		5000	1800	2220	1940	2390	2100	2570	2330	2840
		6000	1990	2460	2150	2650	2400	2930	2580	3160
		7000	2210	2730	2470	3030	2660	3270	2870	3530
		8000	2540	3140	2750	3400	2970	3680	3210	3980
		9000	2840	3540	3080	3840	3330	4170	3610	4530
		10,000	3170	3990	3440	4340	3730	4730	4040	5160
4700	85	Sea Level	920	1140	990	1220	1060	1300	1140	1390
		1000	1010	1250	1080	1340	1170	1430	1250	1530
		2000	1100	1360	1190	1460	1280	1570	1370	1670
		3000	1210	1500	1310	1600	1410	1720	1510	1840
		4000	1340	1650	1440	1770	1550	1900	1670	2030
		5000	1470	1810	1590	1940	1710	2090	1840	2240
		6000	1620	2000	1750	2150	1890	2310	2030	2480
		7000	1800	2210	1940	2380	2090	2560	2260	2760
		8000	1990	2460	2160	2650	2330	2860	2600	3170
		9000	2230	2750	2490	3060	2690	3300	2900	3560
		10,000	2560	3160	2770	3420	3000	3700	3240	4010
4300	81	Sea Level	750	930	800	1000	860	1060	920	1130
		1000	820	1020	880	1090	940	1160	1010	1240
		2000	890	1110	960	1190	1030	1270	1110	1360
		3000	980	1210	1050	1300	1130	1390	1220	1490
		4000	1080	1330	1160	1430	1250	1530	1340	1630
		5000	1180	1460	1270	1560	1370	1680	1470	1790
		6000	1300	1600	1400	1720	1510	1840	1620	1980
		7000	1440	1770	1550	1900	1670	2040	1800	2190
		8000	1590	1960	1720	2100	1850	2260	2000	2430
		9000	1770	2180	1910	2340	2060	2530	2230	2720
		10,000	1960	2420	2120	2610	2290	2810	2560	3120

nent of 55 degrees at 18 knots, you will find the headwind component to be 10 knots. According to the note at the top of the chart,
decrease all distances by 7 percent for each 10 knots of headwind.
Thus 93 percent of 2450 feet is 2278 feet. The correct answer is
No. 3.

Try the following questions using the same charts for practice.

What is the normal takeoff distance for operating conditions D-2?

1. 1,950 ft.
2. 2,153 ft.
3. 2,261 ft.
4. 2,355 ft.

Answer No. 4 is correct.

What is the normal takeoff distance for operating conditions D-3?

1. 3,043 ft.
2. 2,820 ft.
3. 2,597 ft.
4. 2,463 ft.

Answer No. 3 is correct. There is no headwind in this problem, but you must consider the sod runway.

The method for finding landing distance is the same as the technique for finding takeoff distance. Here are some sample questions
for practice.

*What is the ground roll distance for operating conditions V- 1? (See
Fig. 6-6 and Tables 6-9 and 6-10.)*

1. 602 ft.
2. 523 ft.
3. 455 ft.
4. 387 ft.

Answer No. 4 is the best choice.

Table 6-9. Normal Landing Distances and Operating Conditions.

OPERATING CONDITIONS	V-1	V-2	V-3	V-4	V-5	V-6
	NORMAL LANDING DISTANCE					
Weight (lb.)	4,600	5,000	5,000	5,400	4,400	4,200
Pressure Altitude (ft.)	1,500	S/L	S/L	1,000	8,000	6,000
Runway	36	18	9	27R	30	26
Runway Surface Level, Hard/Firm, Dry	Concrete	Asphalt	Sod	Sod	Concrete	Asphalt
Wind Direction/Speed	030°/23	280°/10	150°/16	010°/10	Calm	360°/10
Temperature	32°F	5°F	50°F	41°F	-10°C	5°F
Wing Flap Setting	35°	35°	UP	35°	UP	35°

Table 6-10. Normal Landing Distances.

CONDITIONS:
1. Throttles - IDLE
2. Landing Gear - DOWN
3. Wing Flaps - 35%
4. Cowl Flaps - CLOSE
5. Level, Hard Surface Runway
6. Maximum Braking Effort

NOTE:
1. Increase all distances by 25% of ground run for operation on firm sod runway.
2. When landing with flaps UP, increase the normal approach speed by 12 knots. Expect total landing distance to increase by 35%.
3. Decrease all distances by 3% for each 4 knots headwind. For operations with tailwinds up to 10 knots, increase all distances by 5% for each 2 knots of wind.

WEIGHT-POUNDS	SPEED AT 50-FOOT OBSTACLE KIAS	PRESSURE ALTITUDE - FEET	-20°C (-4°F)		-10°C (14°F)		0°C (32°F)		10°C (50°F)	
			GROUND ROLL - FEET	TOTAL DISTANCE TO CLEAR 50-FOOT OBSTACLE	GROUND ROLL - FEET	TOTAL DISTANCE TO CLEAR 50-FOOT OBSTACLE	GROUND ROLL - FEET	TOTAL DISTANCE TO CLEAR 50-FOOT OBSTACLE	GROUND ROLL - FEET	TOTAL DISTANCE TO CLEAR 50-FOOT OBSTACLE
5400	93	Sea Level	570	1720	590	1740	610	1760	630	1780
		1000	590	1740	610	1760	630	1780	660	1810
		2000	610	1760	630	1780	660	1810	680	1830
		3000	630	1780	660	1810	680	1830	710	1860
		4000	660	1810	680	1830	710	1860	730	1880
		5000	680	1830	710	1860	730	1880	760	1910
		6000	710	1860	730	1880	760	1910	790	1940
		7000	730	1880	760	1910	790	1940	820	1970
		8000	760	1910	790	1940	820	1970	850	2000
		9000	790	1940	820	1970	850	2000	880	2030
		10,000	820	1970	850	2000	890	2040	920	2070
5000	89	Sea Level	480	1630	500	1650	520	1670	540	1690
		1000	500	1650	520	1670	540	1690	560	1710
		2000	520	1670	540	1690	560	1710	580	1730
		3000	530	1680	560	1710	580	1730	600	1750
		4000	550	1700	580	1730	600	1750	620	1770
		5000	580	1730	600	1750	620	1770	640	1790
		6000	600	1750	620	1770	640	1790	670	1820
		7000	620	1770	640	1790	670	1820	690	1840
		8000	640	1790	670	1820	690	1840	720	1870
		9000	670	1820	700	1850	720	1870	750	1900
		10,000	700	1850	720	1870	750	1900	780	1930
4600	86	Sea Level	400	1550	420	1570	430	1580	450	1590
		1000	410	1560	430	1580	450	1600	460	1610
		2000	430	1580	450	1600	460	1610	480	1630
		3000	450	1600	460	1610	480	1630	500	1650
		4000	460	1610	480	1630	500	1650	520	1670
		5000	480	1630	500	1650	520	1670	540	1690
		6000	500	1650	520	1670	540	1690	560	1710
		7000	520	1670	540	1690	560	1710	580	1730
		8000	540	1690	560	1710	580	1730	600	1750
		9000	560	1710	580	1730	600	1750	620	1770
		10,000	580	1730	600	1750	620	1770	650	1800
4200	82	Sea Level	330	1480	340	1490	350	1500	370	1520
		1000	340	1490	350	1500	370	1520	380	1530
		2000	350	1500	370	1520	380	1530	390	1540
		3000	370	1520	380	1530	390	1540	410	1560
		4000	380	1530	390	1540	410	1560	420	1570
		5000	390	1540	410	1560	420	1570	440	1590
		6000	410	1560	420	1570	440	1590	460	1610
		7000	420	1570	440	1590	460	1610	470	1620
		8000	440	1590	460	1610	470	1620	490	1640
		9000	460	1610	480	1630	490	1640	510	1660
		10,000	480	1630	490	1640	510	1660	530	1680

What is the total distance to clear a 50-foot obstacle for operating conditions V-3?

1. 1,589 ft.
2. 1,690 ft.
3. 1,986 ft.
4. 2,681 ft.

Answer No. 4 is the best choice.

Possibly the FAA goes too far on the test with this format of testing. Nonetheless, accelerate/go problems are part of the instrument written exam. Don't ask me why, but as in the previous two sets of problems, the method is the same. Try these for familiarity.

What is the accelerate/go distance for operating conditions H-1? (Use Tables 6-11 and 6-12.)

1. 8,576 ft.
2. 9,013 ft.
3. 10,015 ft.
4. 11,017 ft.

Answer No. 4 is the best choice.

What is the accelerate/go distance for operating conditions H-2?

1. 9,673 ft.
2. 10,430 ft.
3. 11,005 ft.
4. 11,645 ft.

Answer No. 2 is correct.

What is the accelerate/go distance for operating conditions H-3?

1. 2,017 ft.
2. 2,276 ft.
3. 2,460 ft.
4. 2,904 ft.

The correct choice is No. 1.

Now you have accelerate/stop problems to solve. Do them in the same manner as above.

Table 6-11. Operating Conditions and Accelerate/Go Distances.

	ACCELERATE-GO DISTANCE					
OPERATING CONDITIONS	H-1	H-2	H-3	H-4	H-5	H-6
Weight (lb.)	5,500	5,100	4,700	5,300	5,300	4,300
Pressure Altitude (ft.)	4,500	4,000	S/L	2,000	1,000	3,000
Temperature	-10°C	104°F	104°F	5°F	10°C	23°F
Wind Components - knots (+)=HW (-)=TW	-5	Calm	+30	-5	Calm	+15

Table 6-12. Accelerate/Go Distances and Operating Conditions.

CONDITIONS:
1. Power - FULL THROTTLE and 2700 RPM Before Brake Release.
2. Mixtures - Lean for field elevation
3. Wing Flaps - UP.
4. Cowl Flaps - OPEN.
5. Level Hard Surface Dry Runway.
6. Engine Failure At Engine Failure Speed.
7. Propeller Feathered and Landing Gear Retracted During Climb.
8. Maintain Engine Failure Speed Until Clear of Obstacle.

NOTE·
1. If full power is applied without brakes set, distances apply from point where full power is applied.
2. Decrease distance 6% for each 10 knots headwind.
3. Increase distance 2% for each knot of tailwind.
4. Distance in boxes represent rates of climb less than 50 ft/min.

WEIGHT - POUNDS	ENGINE FAILURE - SPEED - KIAS	PRESSURE ALTITUDE - FEET	TOTAL DISTANCE TO CLEAR 50-FOOT OBSTACLE						
			-20°C -4°F	-10°C +14°F	0°C 32°F	+10°C +50°F	+20°C +68°F	+30°C +86°F	+40°C +104°F
5500	92	Sea Level	2600	2850	3120	3450	3840	4320	4950
		1000	3010	3330	3700	4160	4760	5560	6810
		2000	3530	3970	4520	5250	6370	8080	11,540
		3000	4310	4990	5950	7520	10,350	------	------
		4000	5650	7020	9550	15,790	------	------	------
		5000	8470	13,010	------	------	------	------	------
		6000	------	------	------	------	------	------	------
		7000	------	------	------	------	------	------	------
		8000	------	------	------	------	------	------	------
		9000	------	------	------	------	------	------	------
		10,000	------	------	------	------	------	------	------
5100	88	Sea Level	2030	2190	2360	2560	2780	3030	3320
		1000	2280	2470	2690	2940	3220	3540	3940
		2000	2580	2820	3090	3400	3770	4230	4810
		3000	2960	3270	3630	4060	4600	5330	6430
		4000	3490	3910	4430	5110	6130	7620	10,430
		5000	4200	4820	5680	7030	9280	14,630	------
		6000	5350	6500	8480	12,550	------	------	------
		7000	7800	11,240	------	------	------	------	------
		8000	------	------	------	------	------	------	------
		9000	------	------	------	------	------	------	------
		10,000	------	------	------	------	------	------	------
4700	85	Sea Level	1600	1720	1840	1980	2130	2290	2460
		1000	1780	1910	2060	2210	2390	2580	2800
		2000	1980	2130	2300	2490	2700	2930	3200
		3000	2210	2400	2600	2830	3090	3390	3740
		4000	2510	2730	2990	3280	3620	4030	4540
		5000	2860	3140	3460	3850	4320	4930	5820
		6000	3320	3690	4130	4700	5450	6610	8370
		7000	3960	4500	5200	6190	7820	10,780	------
		8000	4990	5920	7350	10,020	16,800	------	------
		9000	7040	9510	15,370	------	------	------	------
		10,000	13,110	------	------	------	------	------	------
4300	81	Sea Level	1270	1360	1450	1550	1650	1760	1890
		1000	1400	1500	1600	1710	1830	1960	2100
		2000	1540	1650	1760	1890	2030	2180	2340
		3000	1700	1820	1960	2110	2270	2440	2640
		4000	1890	2040	2190	2370	2560	2770	3020
		5000	2100	2270	2460	2670	2900	3170	3470
		6000	2360	2570	2790	3050	3340	3690	4100
		7000	2690	2940	3220	3550	3950	4430	5110
		8000	3110	3430	3810	4280	4860	5720	6850
		9000	3690	4150	4710	5460	6610	8330	11,760
		10,000	4490	5190	6160	7730	10,510	------	------

Table 6-13. Accelerate/Stop Distances and Operating Conditions.

OPERATING CONDITIONS	ACCELERATE-STOP DISTANCE					
	G-1	G-2	G-3	G-4	G-5	G-6
Weight (lb.)	4,300	4,500	4,700	4,900	5,100	5,500
Pressure Altitude (ft.)	7,500	4,000	3,000	1,000	2,500	8,500
Temperature	104°F	86°F	59°F	41°F	5°F	40°C
Wind Components - knots (+)=HW (-)=TW	+8	-2	+4	-4	Calm	+8

What is the accelerate/stop distance for operating conditions G-1? (Use Fig. 6-6 and Tables 6-13 and 6-14.)

1. 3,798 ft.
2. 4,040 ft.
3. 4,122 ft.
4. 4,282 ft.

The best choice is No. 1.

What is the accelerate/stop distance for operating conditions G-2?

1. 3,078 ft.
2. 3,240 ft.
3. 3,375 ft.
4. 3,402 ft.

Number 4 is the correct choice.

What is the accelerate/stop distance for operating conditions G-3?
1. 2,988 ft.
2. 3,080 ft.
3. 3,160 ft.
4. 3,260 ft.

Choice No. 1 is the closest answer.

Table 6-14. Accelerate/Stop Distances.

CONDITIONS:
1. Power - FULL THROTTLE and 2700 RPM Before Brake Release.
2. Mixtures - LEAN for field elevation
3. Wing Flaps - UP.
4. Cowl Flaps - OPEN.
5. Level, Hard Surface, Dry Runway.
6. Engine Failure at Engine Failure Speed.
7. Idle Power and Heavy Braking After Engine Failure.

NOTE:
1. If full power is applied without brakes set, distances apply from point where full power is applied.
2. Decrease distance 3% for each 4 knots headwind.
3. Increase distance 5% for each 2 knots tailwind.

WEIGHT - POUNDS	ENGINE FAILURE SPEED - KIAS	PRESSURE ALTITUDE - FEET	TOTAL DISTANCE - FEET						
			-20°C -4°F	-10°C +14°F	0°C 32°F	+10°C +50°F	+20°C +68°F	+30°C +86°F	+40°C +104°F
5500	92	Sea Level	3020	3190	3370	3550	3740	3930	4120
		1000	3220	3400	3590	3790	3990	4210	4490
		2000	3430	3630	3830	4050	4340	4570	4820
		3000	3660	3880	4100	4400	4650	4910	5180
		4000	3920	4160	4480	4730	5000	5290	5590
		5000	4200	4530	4810	5090	5390	5700	6030
		6000	4590	4880	5180	5490	5820	6170	6530
		7000	4950	5270	5600	5940	6310	6700	7110
		8000	5360	5710	6070	6460	6870	7310	7780
		9000	5830	6210	6630	7060	7530	8020	8560
		10,000	6330	6770	7230	7720	8250	8810	9420
5100	88	Sea Level	2540	2680	2830	2980	3140	3300	3470
		1000	2710	2860	3020	3180	3350	3530	3710
		2000	2880	3050	3220	3390	3580	3770	3970
		3000	3070	3250	3440	3630	3830	4040	4330
		4000	3290	3480	3680	3900	4190	4420	4660
		5000	3520	3730	3950	4250	4500	4750	5020
		6000	3770	4010	4320	4580	4850	5130	5430
		7000	4060	4390	4660	4950	5240	5560	5890
		8000	4470	4750	5050	5360	5690	6050	6420
		9000	4840	5160	5490	5840	6220	6610	7030
		10,000	5250	5600	5970	6370	6790	7230	7710
4700	85	Sea Level	2110	2230	2350	2470	2600	2740	2870
		1000	2250	2370	2500	2640	2770	2920	3070
		2000	2390	2520	2660	2810	2960	3120	3280
		3000	2540	2690	2840	3000	3160	3340	3510
		4000	2720	2880	3040	3210	3390	3580	3780
		5000	2900	3080	3260	3440	3640	3840	4130
		6000	3110	3300	3500	3700	3910	4210	4450
		7000	3340	3550	3760	3990	4300	4550	4820
		8000	3600	3830	4070	4390	4660	4940	5230
		9000	3900	4230	4490	4770	5070	5380	5710
		10,000	4300	4580	4870	5180	5510	5860	6240
4300	81	Sea Level	1730	1820	1920	2020	2120	2230	2340
		1000	1830	1940	2040	2150	2260	2380	2500
		2000	1950	2060	2170	2290	2410	2530	2660
		3000	2070	2190	2310	2440	2570	2710	2850
		4000	2210	2340	2470	2610	2750	2900	3060
		5000	2360	2500	2640	2790	2950	3110	3280
		6000	2520	2680	2830	2990	3160	3340	3530
		7000	2710	2870	3040	3220	3410	3600	3880
		8000	2910	3090	3280	3470	3680	3970	4200
		9000	3140	3340	3550	3760	4070	4310	4570
		10,000	3390	3610	3830	4150	4410	4680	4970

Chapter 7

Weather

It is incredible how many pilots and instrument students hate to study weather. It is also incredible to me how little they know after they have studied. Weather systems follow guidelines or laws of motion and physics. Even though the predictability of weather is not very accurate on the long scale, it is very easy to predict on the short term. The FAA dwells on six areas that pertain to weather or weather facilities. These areas are: Fundamentals of Weather, IFR Weather Hazards, Aviation Weather Forecasts, Weather Tables and Conversion Graphs, and Weather Facilities. I will discuss each one carefully and sample questions will follow each.

Hopefully, you will learn a little in addition to passing the test. Remember, instrument flying is weather flying. If you are not interested in learning about the weather, then you will be a dangerous pilot, hazardous to all that share the airspace with you, and someday a cloud will spit you out. Every instrument pilot should know how to best deal with weather situations he gets into, as well as avoiding them in the first place.

FUNDAMENTALS OF WEATHER

The first gamut of questions are on pressure altitude and its relation to true altitude. *Pressure altitude* is the altitude the altimeter indicates when set to the standard pressure at sea level, which is 29.92 inches of mercury. *True altitude* is the exact height above mean sea level. Using these definitions, reason your way through the following question.

Under what condition will true altitude be lower than indicated altitude with an altimeter setting of 29.92 even with an accurate altimeter?

1. In colder than standard air temperature.
2. In warmer than standard air temperature.
3. When density altitude is higher than indicated altitude.
4. Under higher than standard pressure at standard air temperature.

Density altitude affects airplane performance but not altimeter indication, therefore answers Nos. 1, 2, and 3 are not correct. Answer No. 4 is correct, because whenever the atmospheric pressure is higher than the altimeter setting, the altimeter reads high. Hence, the true altitude will be lower than indicated.

To make the point clear that density altitude is not the same as pressure altitude answer the following question.

Under what condition is pressure altitude and density altitude the same value?

1. At sea level, when the temperature of O° F.
2. When the altimeter has *no* installation error.
3. When the altimeter setting is 29.92.
4. At standard temperature.

Answer No. 4 is correct, because density altitude varies as to temperature. Only when the temperature is standard does pressure altitude and density altitude coincide.

Another pilot and I were discussing an ILS approach. I asked him if he had ever noticed that in general terms, as one proceeds down the glide slope and localizer, that correction to the left becomes more necessary as the aircraft gets lower. As we picked the possibilities apart, it became evident that the wind is deflected due to surface friction of the earth. As one climbs, the winds come from more to the right. A descent means the winds swing around to the left.

Winds at 5,000 feet AGL on a particular flight are southwesternly

*while most of the surface winds are southerly. This difference in direc-
tion is primarily due to . . .*

1. a stronger pressure gradient at higher altitudes.
2. stronger Coriolis force at the surface.
3. friction between the wind and the surface.
4. the influence of pressure systems at the lower altitudes.

Answer No. 3 is the only answer referring to surface friction. It must be correct.

Frost forms during the cool and cold seasons. Frost adhering to wings interrupts smooth airflow over the airfoil. Frost is formed by a process of *sublimation*, the process by which water vapor passes directly from the form as a gas to ice crystals without passing through the liquid state. Nothing falls from the sky to produce the frost. To simply say that frost is frozen dew is incorrect. Check out the next question. Three answers are found to be incorrect right away, according to the above information.

What conditions result in the formation of frost?

1. The freezing of dew.
2. The collecting surface's temperature is at or below freezing and small droplets of moisture fall on the collecting surface.
3. The temperature of the collecting surface is at or below the dew point of the adjacent air and the dew point is below freezing.
4. Small drops of moisture falling on the collecting surface when the surrounding air temperature is at or below freezing.

The correct choice is obviously No. 3. If small drops of moisture fell to make frost it wouldn't be called frost, it would be called freezing drizzle. The importance of knowing about frost is not necessarily from the preflight aspect, although that is important. Frost may form in flight also. Whenever an aircraft is descending from a cold air mass to warmer air below and the skin is chilled below the dew point, frost may form.

Other forms of moisture may be encountered in clouds. The temperature at your altitude determines the type of moisture you will encounter. If it is below freezing, some sort of freezing precipitation or structural ice may be present.

You encounter wet snow during a cross-country flight. What does this indicate regarding temperatures in the area?

1. You are flying from a warm air mass into a cold air mass.
2. You are in an "inversion" with colder air below.
3. The temperature is above freezing at your altitude.
4. The temperature is above freezing at higher altitudes.

Deductive reasoning is the best way to solve questions like this one. Generally, the FAA has two bad choices and two good ones. Eliminate the two bad ones and reason out the good ones.

Number 1 is a bad choice, because it talks in terms of transitioning from one air mass to another. The reason this is a bad choice is that one may fly through several types of precipitation, not just wet snow. That leaves you with three answers to choose from now.

Number 2 is a bad choice. Though the aircraft could be in an inversion, the question does not give enough information to draw that conclusion. If you chose number 2, you are reading too much into the question.

Number 3 is the best choice. Wet snow is a result of snow warming and starting to melt: therefore, answer No. 3 is the most accurate statement.

Number 4 may be correct, however, it is not most correct.

The FAA also looks at other types of precipitation one might encounter during flight. Several of these pertain to ice pellets. Ice pellets are formed by rain being carried aloft or falling into a much cooler atmospheric layer below. The FAA book, *Aviation Weather,* the source for weather questions, states emphatically that where ice pellets are falling, there is freezing rain somewhere above.

The presence of ice pellets at the surface is evidence that . . .

1. a cold front has passed.
2. there are thunderstorms in the area.
3. temperatures are above freezing at some higher altitude.
4. you can climb to a higher altitude without encountering more than light icing.

The only good choice is No. 3. The temperatures must be above freezing at some higher altitude. Remember, ice pellets begin as rain, then fall into a much cooler layer, or they can be carried back aloft, usually at great heights where they freeze and fall through the rain layer into below-freezing temperatures below the rain layer.

Temperatures largely determine how much water vapor the air can hold. Warm air can hold more moisture than cold air, and there is a point when the warm air is cooled that the water vapor becomes visible as clouds or fog. This point where a mass of air reaches its saturation point is called the *dew point*.

The term relative humidity fits in this discussion at this point. Most likely, everyone has read about the importance of the temperature, dew-point spread. The "spread," as it is known, is only of value for predicting fog and not precipitation.

The amount of water vapor which air can hold largely depends on . . .

1. the dewpoint.
2. air temperature.
3. stability of air.
4. relative humidity.

According to the FAA publication on weather, No. 2 is the correct choice.

CLOUDS

The next area we will look at is the area of atmospheric stability. Fundamentally, identification of stable or unstable air is the focal point of the FAA's questions. Stable air is generally associated with stratiform clouds. *Stratus* clouds are those that are layered. During stable atmospheric conditions such as slow moving high pressure areas, the visibility is poor or restricted due to haze and pollutants. Whenever our cities and the National Weather Service issue air stagnation advisories, the air is in a stable situation.

Stratus clouds occur in stable air. The type of icing in these clouds is generally *rime*. The reason for this is the relatively small drops of moisture of which the clouds are made. Because there is little or no lifting in stratiform clouds, large droplets of water cannot be held aloft. For this reason, rain in heavy amounts is hardly ever received from pure stratus clouds. Stratus clouds are sometimes forced upslope. This happens in mountainous areas. Whenever they are forced upslope, they tend to retain their horizontal stability. Thus, the rule is: stable air and associated weather conditions tend to resist change and remains stable.

The converse of all that is said of stable air is true of unstable air. *Cumuliform* types of clouds are generally associated with unstable air masses. Cumulus clouds are those that are developed vertically. Generally, visibility is good in unstable air conditions, because the air mass is in constant movement.

Cumulus clouds are indicative of unstable air masses. The type of icing in these clouds is generally clear or a mixture of rime and clear ice. Because lifting is great in unstable air, the droplets of moisture that form the cumuliform clouds are large in comparison of those of stratus clouds. Whenever cumuliform clouds precipitate, the rain or snow is in moderate or heavy amounts. A general rule of thumb is that it takes about 4,000 feet of cloud thickness to produce at least moderate precipitation. Stratus clouds rarely achieve that sort of thickness. Whenever cumulus clouds are forced upslope, they continue to develop vertically and become orographic-type thunderstorms.

Now, let's apply our new found knowledge to some questions on air mass stability. As before, these questions come from the FAA written exam.

What are the characteristics of unstable air?

Visibility	Type of Precipitation	Type of Clouds
1. Poor	Intermittent	Cumulus
2. Poor	Steady	Stratus
3. Good	Showers	Cumulus
4. Good	Steady	Stratus

Using the process of elimination technique on weather questions can often be very helpful. Generally, you can count on the FAA to give at least two answers out of every four to be close. Two can be thrown out, and then you can choose between the remaining two answers. In this question, finding the correct one is easy if you refer to the previous discussion. First, begin with unstable air. Then, ask yourself, what cloud type is indicative of unstable air? Cumulus. There are only two answers that contain cumulus as a choice—Nos. 1 and 3. The type precipitation is not the best clue, so use the visibility description. Is visibility good or poor in unstable air condition? It is usually good. Therefore, answer

No. 3 must be correct, because it contains the correct cloud type and visibility.

What type of clouds will be formed if very stable moist air is forced upslope?

1. Vertical clouds with increasing height.
2. Layerlike clouds with little vertical development.
3. First layer clouds and then vertical clouds.
4. First vertical clouds and then layer clouds.

The target question pertains to the type of cloud formation in stable air conditions when that air is forced upslope. As discussed, the stratus layer, when forced up a mountain slope, maintains its stability and remains layered. Therefore, answer No. 2 is the correct choice.

A temperature inversion forms . . .
1. only in summer.
2. only in winter.
3. develop convective turbulence.
4. a stable layer of air.

An indication of stable air is a uniform decrease in temperature as the airplane climbs, called the *dry adiabatic lapse rate*. This can be noticed by watching the outside air temperature (OAT) gauge as you climb-out. Another indication that may occur would be a decrease in temperature, then an increase in temperature followed by continued decrease. This is called a temperature *inversion* and is sometimes present in stable air. An inversion forms a sort of stable boundary layer and can form anytime of the year. Therefore, answer No. 4 is the only possible choice.

One more question on air stability to check yourself on this subject and your process of elimination technique.

What are the characteristics of stable air?

Visibility	Type of Precipitation	Type of Clouds
1. Good	Showers	Cumulus
2. Poor	Intermittent	Cumulus
3. Good	Steady	Stratus
4. Poor	Steady	Stratus

Choice No. 4 is the correct one. Visibility is generally poor in stable or stagnant conditions. Stratus clouds are the typical cloud type in stable air masses.

Some of the weather questions will invariably be on identification of clouds. In order to answer these questions, you will need to know about their appearance, as well as certain characteristics as they apply to flight through a particular cloud type.

Fundamentally, there are only three cloud types. Those are cirrus, stratus, and cumulus. We will examine each one separately, beginning with cirrus. *Cirrus* clouds are always high clouds. They form at altitudes above 25,000 feet. The temperatures at those altitudes are usually well below freezing. As a result, cirrus clouds are made of small ice crystals instead of the water droplets. Because

Fig. 7-1. Fair weather cumulus clouds. The dark bottoms are due to the bottoms being concave and shaded from the sun.

137

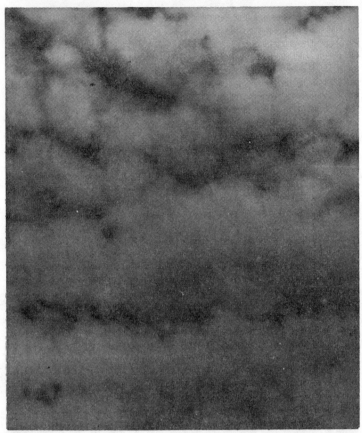

Fig. 7-2. Altocumulus clouds are typical of moist unstable air at the middle altitudes.

clouds of this type are made of ice crystals, flights through them result in extremely negligible amounts of airframe icing. Simply stated, the ice particles bounce off the aircrafts structure.

Stratus clouds are the layered type in air mass stability. Generally flat in appearance, they often form broken or overcast ceilings.

Cumulus clouds, on the other hand, are billowy and fluffy. Often times, cumulus clouds (shown in Fig. 7-1) are white and majestic looking. Small cumulus clouds, though, have a knack for growing to immense size and raising all sorts of havoc on summer afternoons. Generally, they are thought of as an indication of convective activity. One can think of a cumulus cloud as the visual end of a rising column of air.

The three main types of clouds may be further divided into three categories according to altitude. (See Figs. 7-2 and 7-3). Low stratus or cumulus are described simply as stratus or cumulus. Whenever these clouds form at altitudes from 8,000 to 25,000 feet they become middle clouds. The word *alto* is then added as a prefix. For instance, a cumulus cloud with a base at about 15,000 feet AGL is called *altocumulus*. There are no altocirrus clouds. The word cirrus refers to high clouds only. There are *altostratus*, however.

The prefix "cirro" is added to clouds above the 25,000-foot level. (See Figs. 7-4 and 7-5). Twenty-five thousand feet is not a hard and fast rule for determining the break over point. As with the middle clouds, there are *cirrostratus* as well as *cirrocumulus*. Don't forget, there are plain old cirrus also.

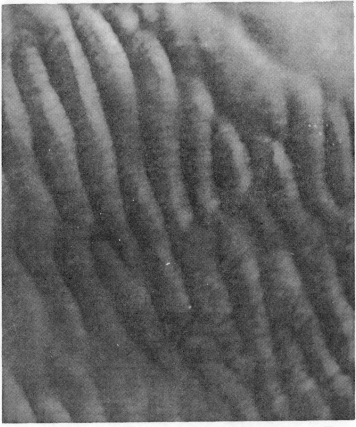

Fig. 7-3. Altostratus clouds are layered and have little vertical extent. These have taken on a rolled appearance, probably due to turbulence aloft.

Fig. 7-4. High cirrus clouds. Cirrus clouds are generally made of ice crystals. Notice that they are somewhat above the jet contrail.

Fig. 7-5. Cirrocumulus clouds. These are indicative of moist unstable air aloft and usually precede fronts by as much as 24 hours.

A middle cloud that is paid particular attention is the *alto-cumulus standing lenticular* (ACSL), generally known as a lenticular cloud. When there is sufficient moisture to form these, they stand downwind from a mountain ridge. They seem to be good for gliders but not much use to power aircraft. Lenticular clouds are indicative of turbulence, especially when a rotor cloud is visible below the downwind edge of one.

Which family of clouds is least likely to contribute to structural icing on an aircraft?

1. Low clouds.
2. Middle clouds.
3. High clouds.
4. Clouds with extensive vertical development.

Because high clouds of the cirrus type are made of small ice crystals that don't adhere very well to the airfoil, structural icing is less. Then choice No. 3 must be correct.

The presence of standing lenticular altocumulus clouds is a good indication of:

1. heavy rain.
2. very strong turbulence.
3. heavy icing conditions.
4. an approaching storm.

Lenticular clouds are good indications of turbulence. Seldom if ever are they sources of precipitation. Icing in them generally would be only moderate in nature. Therefore, you can draw the conclusion that answer No. 2 is correct.

Now, here's a curve thrown at you:

The suffix "nimbus," used in naming clouds, means:

1. a cloud with extensive vertical development.
2. a rain cloud.
3. a middle cloud containing ice pellet.
4. an accumulation of clouds.

If you are up on your Latin, it was probably easy. Or, if you have been studying clouds elsewhere, it should have been no problem. But if you don't know, here's the answer. The word "nimbus" means rain cloud. As well, the "nimbo" when used as a prefix means rain; therefore, answer No. 2 is correct.

WINDS

Although there are not very many questions on frontal activity, every applicant should be familiar. After all, the written test is a drop in the bucket of necessary information. What happens when you need to fly to the other side of a front for real? Knowing the answer to the question on the written isn't much armament.

One thing is common to all fronts whether they be warm, cold, or occluded. When a front passes, there is a definite wind shift. One of the oddest things I have ever seen involved a frontal passage. I was on a scheduled flight to an airport in western Oklahoma. As we approached the airport, which is an uncontrolled field, we faced a dilemma as to which way to land. West of the airport we could see a farmer plowing his field and the dust was blowing to the south, indicating a north wind. East of the airport the dust was blowing north, indicating a southerly wind. On the south end of the airport, the wind sock showed a west wind, and the wind tetrahedron on the north end of the aerodrome indicated the wind was from the east. We had wind indications in all four major directions. What we wound up doing was flying a downwind to the north and landed south. The wind was almost calm on the ground and in the process of switching from south to north. Our preflight weather briefing told us of a weak cold front in the area. After landing at Altus, Oklahoma, we were positive of its position.

Besides a wind shift, a pilot can usually notice a temperature change. Also, an interesting fact is that when flying through a front of any kind in the northern hemisphere, in any direction, a correction to the right is needed when penetrating the frontal line.

Which weather phenomenon is always associated with the passage of a frontal system?

1. A wind shift.
2. An abrupt decrease in pressure.
3. Clouds, either ahead or behind the front.
4. An abrupt decrease in temperature.

Answer No. 1 is the best choice, although all of the others are certainly true at some time with certain types of fronts.

In recent years, since the Eastern Airlines crash at Kennedy International Airport in New York during a thunderstorm, the FAA has put a great deal more emphasis on *wind shear*. To begin with, wind shear may occur at any altitude. Wind shear can either be a change in wind direction or even an abrupt change in windspeed gradient. Many times, when crossing through a temperature inversion, one may notice rough air. Often, a wind shear exists at the inversion in the form of either wind shift, or change in wind speed gradient, or both. The old saw that everything that goes up must come down applies to wind shear most aptly. For every updraft there is a downdraft. That means that wind shear may also exist in a vertical direction. That is one thing that makes flying through a thunderstorm so very dangerous.

Where does wind shear occur?

1. Only at higher altitudes, usually in the vicinity of jetstreams.
2. At any level, and it can exist in both a horizontal and vertical direction.
3. Primarily at lower altitudes in the vicinity of mountain waves.
4. Only in the vicinity of thunderstorms.

Answer No. 2 is correct as discussed above. Try the next one; it's tricky.

Hazardous wind shear is commonly encountered near the ground in the vicinity of thunderstorms and with warm afternoon temperatures . . .

1. during periods when the wind velocity is stronger than 35 knots.
2. near mountain valleys when the lapse rate is greater than normal.
3. during periods of strong low level temperature inversion.
4. on the windward side of a hill or mountain.

Choice No. 3 is correct. Wind shear may occur after sunset at low levels whenever the air close to the ground calms down below an inversion. The speed of the warm air above the inversion may be 30 knots or so. The net result, if descending or climbing downwind through the inversion, is a loss of airspeed. This may be critical, because in descents just prior to landing, or in a climb out, airspeeds are already near the stall, and any loss of airspeed may induce a stall.

Addressing the last question in particular, it is interesting to note that the FAA's professional test writers have clouded the target question with extraneous information. Pick your way carefully through the question, comparing the answers with the information. If you don't find an answer that directly applies to the way question reads, then that statement is extraneous.

IFR WEATHER HAZARDS

It seems that when flying on the gauges, if you don't have to deal with thunderstorms, then you are in the ice. There are three basic types of structural icing. They are *rime, clear*, and *frost*. We have already discussed frost, so we will dwell on the other types for the time being.

Rime ice is generally found in stratus-type clouds. It has the appearance of being milky and rough-textured, sort of like the frost that forms in nonfrost-free freezers. Rime ice usually builds upon itself after it starts. As a result, the ice builds into the slip stream from the leading edge of the wing. It builds this way due to the small size of the water droplets. Moreover, the temperature is cold enough to cause it to freeze quickly and not spread back into the slip stream over the aircraft surface.

Clear ice forms in a different environment. More often than not, the aircraft is in cumulus-type clouds where the water droplets are comparatively larger. A larger drop takes more time to freeze and, as a result, spreads out and forms over more surface. The large size of the droplets also plays a part in the appearance of the ice. As you know, ice cubes are not always crystal clear and neither is clear ice. In real flight conditions, often you will find a mixture of clear and rime.

What are the characteristics of rime ice, and what conditions are most favorable for its formation?

1. Opaque, rough appearance, tending to spread back over an aircraft surface. Most frequently encountered in cumuliform clouds at temperatures slightly below freezing.
2. Smooth appearance and builds forward from leading surfaces into a sharp edge. Most common in cumuliform clouds at temperatures of −20 degrees C. to −25 degrees C.
3. Milky, granular appearance, forming on leading edges, and ac-

cumulating forward into the airstream. Stratiform clouds and temperatures of – 10 degrees C. to – 20 degrees C. are most conducive to its formation.

4. Transparent appearance and tendency to take the shape of the surface on which it freezes. Stratiform clouds and temperatures only slightly below freezing promote its formation.

At first glance, answer Nos. 1 and 2 appear correct; however, they both have descriptions of both clear and rime icing. Choice No. 3 is the only correct answer.

In which conditions would you most likely encounter clear structural icing, and how would it normally appear?

1. Cummuliform clouds; large water droplets; temperatures between 0 and – 15 degrees C. Appears smooth and tends to spread back over an aircraft surface.
2. Stratiform clouds; small water droplets; temperatures between – 10 degrees C. and – 20 degrees C. Appears granular and tends to accumulate forward into the airstream.
3. Cumuliform clouds; small water droplets; temperatures – 20 degrees C. to – 25 degrees C. Appears transparent and tends to take the shape of the surface on which it freezes.
4. Stratiform clouds; large water droplets; temperatures well below freezing. Appears opaque and builds forward from leading surfaces into a sharp edge.

The two obvious choices describing cumuliform clouds are not that obvious. The temperatures may be confusing, but 0 degrees C. to – 15 degrees C. is about the right temperature for ice formation. The temperatures mentioned in choice No. 3 are a little too cold. The give away is in the phrase "large water droplets." That phrase is in answer No. 1, and that is the correct phrase.

Flying through thunderstorms is a bone jarring, lip biting, harrowing experience. See Fig. 7-6. Flying is usually fun until you get yourself mixed up with the turbulence of a thunderstorm. Thunderstorms can build anywhere. They are generally classified as to their occurrence. When a thunderstorm is independent of frontal activity and is built by the thermal uplift, then it is called an *air mass thunderstorm*. Most times these types of thunderstorms can be circumnavigated. At times, however, even air mass storms will band into a line. This frequently happens in the gulf states and

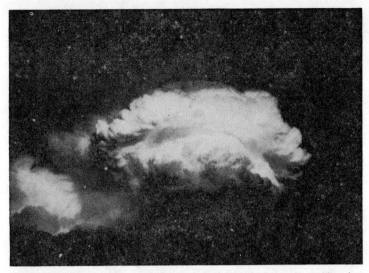

Fig. 7-6. Fighting a cumulonimbus cloud in its mature stage is exciting, but extremely dangerous.

occasionally in the plain states. Whenever these storms are characterized by the frequent lightning and roll clouds, the storms are intense. Experts have found that more intense storms have proportionally intense lightning displays.

Fast moving cold fronts generate squall lines. A cold front is similar to an airfoil moving through the air. Out in front of the wing, a shock wave builds up as speed approaches the speed of sound. Though a cold front does not move nearly so fast it operates by the same physical law that sets squall lines in motions. A squall line may precede the actual cold front by 300 miles. The National Weather Service defines squall line thunderstorms as the most intense producers of severe weather. Don't punch squall lines as a rule, wait for them to pass or go around one end.

Probably the most difficult type of thunderstorm flying comes with warm fronts. Often, when flying a warm front, you are in Instrument Meterological Conditions (IMC). On the gauges, in other words. Unless you have radar available to you, it is extremely easy to blunder into an embedded thunderstorm. Though warm front thunderstorms are not usually as severe as other types, they will give you a bad ride anyway.

Now that I have covered the main points the FAA deems important enough to quiz you on, let's try a few.

146

What visible signs indicate extreme turbulence in thunderstorms?

1. Cumulonimbus clouds, very frequent lightning, and roll clouds.
2. Base of the clouds close to surface, heavy rain, and hail.
3. Low ceiling and visibility, hail, and precipitation static.
4. Lightning, roll clouds, low ceilings and visibility, and precipitation static.

The best choice is No 1. Although low ceilings and visibilities occur with thunderstorms, they don't always. They are not indicators of turbulence either. Roll clouds are the best indicator. These clouds form at the eddies between updraft and downdrafts.

What is indicated when a current SIGMET forecasts "embedded thunderstorms?"

1. Thunderstorms have been visually sighted.
2. Severe thunderstorm are embedded within a squall line.
3. Thunderstorms are dissipating and present no serious problem to IFR flight.
4. Thunderstorms are obscured by massive cloud layers and cannot be seen.

Remember, that SIGMET stands for significant meterological advisory. Many thunderstorms are sighted everyday without the NWS issuing a SIGMET. Thus, answer No. 1 is incorrect. Squall lines *are* thunderstorms; there is nothing embedded about it. So, No. 2 is not the right choice. Number 3 is ridiculous after what we just said about SIGMETS. That leaves us with one choice left— No. 4. It is the correct choice.

Here's an easy one. The FAA really gives you a break on this.

Which weather phenomenon is always associated with a thunderstorm?

1. Lightning.
2. Heavy rain showers.
3. Supercooled raindrops.
4. Hail.

Number 1 is correct. After ail, you can't have thunder without lightning.

What conditions are necessary for the formation of a thunderstorm?

1. Frontal activity, cumulus clouds, and sufficient moisture.
2. Cumulus clouds, unbalance of static electricity, and turbulence.
3. Sufficient heat, moisture, and electricity.
4. Lifting action, unstable air, and sufficient moisture.

It is important to understand what causes thunderstorms. Cumulus clouds and electricity are prerequisites of thunderstorms. Therefore, answer Nos. 1, 2 and 3 are all incorrect. Number 4 has the proper ingredients for thunderstorm generation and is the correct answer.

Fog is the most common IFR hazard. There are three main types of fog. *Radiation fog* is formed whenever warm, moist air, on a calm night, moves over cooler ground. Usually, the ground has cooled and then cools the air next to it.

Another type of fog is *advection fog*. This type usually forms whenever moist air moves over colder ground or water. Most commonly, it forms along coastal areas. It is sometimes called "sea fog." The distinguishing feature of advection fog is the fact that light winds are needed to produce it. The more the wind blows, up to around 15 knots, the layer thickens. When the wind speeds are stronger than 15 knots, the layer moves up and becomes a low stratus deck.

Upslope fog is the third major kind. This fog forms when winds carrying moist air upslope cools adiabatically. It is most commonly found on the eastern slopes of the Rockies and less frequently east of the Appalachian mountains.

What types of fog depend upon a wind in order to exist?

1. Radiation fog and ice fog.
2. Precipitation fog and steam fog.
3. Upslope fog and downslope fog.
4. Advection fog and upslope fog.

As discussed, advection fog as well as upslope fog needs a wind for formation. That leaves only answer No. 4 for the correct choice.

At times, fog is prevalent in industrial areas because of . . .

1. atmospheric stabilization around cities.

2. an abundance of condensation nuclei from combustion products.
3. the high rate of evaporation from water used by factories.
4. a high concentration of steam from industrial plants.

Pollutants have become a problem and part and parcel of our daily lives. Though various gases are released to the atmosphere by various type of industries, it is not the gases that cause fog. The abundance of particulate matter allows moisture to condense more readily. Answer No. 2 is the correct choice for this question.

AVIATION WEATHER OBSERVATION AND REPORTS

The written exam will include questions on reading and interpreting weather reports. Included in this chapter is a legend to decipher the hourly sequence reports and coded *Pireps*. Once the order in which they are given is memorized, the codes for various sky conditions and obstructions to visibility must be learned.

There seems to be no easy way to memorize the order for hourly sequence reports. The question "IS VOST A DWARC?" may help if you do have problems. I stands for the identifier of the reporting station. S is for sky and ceiling. V and O are for visibility and any obstructions. T is temperature. A is and. D represents dewpoint. W is wind direction and velocity. A is the altimeter setting. R is runway visual range. C is a coded Pirep. This method may not be the best method, but it will work.

The most easily confused symbols belong in the sky and ceiling category of an hourly sequence report. The symbol X means sky obscured. When a minus sign appears with it, the − X means partially obscured. You can remember this in this way. If you throw your hands up before your face they usually cross. That would obscure the sky from your vision. The symbol W stands for indefinite. If you remember what the X means, you don't need to remember the W.

What is the visibility, weather, and obstruction to vision at MDW? (See Table 7-1.)

1. Visibility 11 miles, occasionally two miles, with rain + fog.
2. 11 miles visibility, except when rain + fog reduce it to two miles.
3. Visibility one and one-half miles, heavy rain, and fog.
4. Visibility one and one-half miles, rain, and heavy fog.

Table 7-1. Question Reference.

```
INK CLR 15 106/77/63/1112G18/000
BOI 150 SCT 30 181/62/42/1304/015
LAX 7 SCT 250 SCT 6HK 129/60/59/2504/991
    LAX 6/38
MDW SP -X M7 OVC 11/2R+F 990/63/61/3205/
    980/RF2 RB12
JFK SP W5 X 1/2F 180/68/64/1804/006/R04RVR
    22V30 TWR VSBY1/4
```

Answer Nos. 3 and 4 appear to be the best two answers available. Answer No. 3 refers to heavy rain, this also refers to the + between the R and the F. Answer No. 4 uses the description heavy fog. You can eliminate the incorrect one right away by using common sense. Fog is not heavy. It weighs very little. Rain, however, can be heavy. The plus sign will always follow the entity that it reinforces.

Identify the wind conditions at JFK. (See Table 7-1.)

1. 360 degrees at 6 knots.
2. 180 degrees at 4 knots.
3. 040 degrees at 22 variable to 30 knots.
4. 040 degrees at 18 knots.

The wind is always given in two digits for the direction and two digits for velocity. The numbers 1804 mean wind is from the south 180 degrees. The velocity is 14 knots or 4 knots. If the velocity was greater then ten knots it would be represented like this: 1814/180 degrees at 14 knots. Choice No. 2 is the correct answer. (See Fig. 7-7).

Where did the BE55 encounter icing conditions? (See Table 7-2.)

1. Over MRB VOR at 8,000 feet.
2. On a flight from MRB to PIT at 8,000 feet.
3. On a flight from MRB to PIT at 3,500 to 6,000 feet.
4. Over MRB VOR from 3,500 to 6,000 feet.

Using the Pirep legend, most of the included Pirep can be deciphered. The problem with this question is that the answer is not readily obvious. The icing was encountered from the 3,500- foot

PIREP

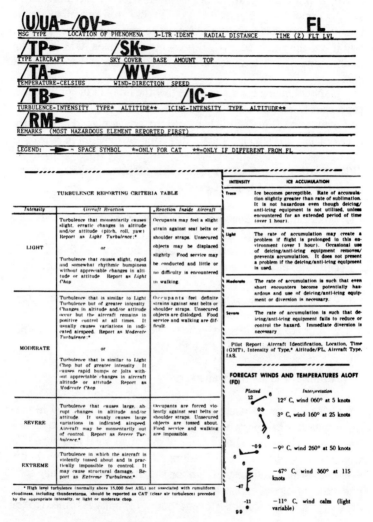

Fig. 7-7. Pilot reports are coded when they are distributed. The legend will enable you to read them accurately.

level up through 6,000 feet. The Pirep was made over MRB enroute to PIT. You must assume that MRB is a VOR because the Pirep says over MRB. Answer No. 4 is the best answer having the proper altitudes and the word "over."

Radar Summary charts can be a great aid in planning long cross-country jaunts. Although areas of precipitation are always on the move, a pilot can gain valuable information. That information usually applies to the expanse of the precip area as well as the intensity. Included is a chart similar to the one you will have on the test if not the same one. NE represents no echoes. OM is out for maintenance. Let's look at a couple of questions and decipher the chart.

In the following questions, note that the number of contour lines represent the intensity of the echo. Refer to the key for an intensity evaluation (Fig. 7-8). Also, note the arrow placed outside the areas of precip, which indicate direction of movement.

What weather conditions are depicted in the area indicated by arrow A on the Radar Summary Chart 7-9?

1. Moderate to strong echoes; echo tops 30,000 ft. MSL; line movement toward the northwest.
2. Weak to moderate echoes; average echo bases 30,000 ft. MSL; cell movement toward the southeast; rain showers with thunder.
3. Moderate echoes; echo bases 3,000 ft. MSL; limited cell movement; rain showers.
4. Strong to very strong echoes; echo tops 30,000 ft. MSL; thundershowers and rain showers.

Number 4 is the best answer.

One of the most used, and probably the handiest aid in preflight weather briefings and flight planning, is the weather depiction chart. This chart shows areas of marginal VFR and pure IFR weather. In addition to cloud ceiling, it also depicts the visibility. A legend is included for you right on the depiction chart. The solid line indicates areas of instrument conditions. The scalloped line indicates area of marginal VFR conditions. Visibility is printed to the

Table 7-2. Question Reference.

```
PIREP

UA/OV MRB-PIT 1600 FL080/TP BE55/SK 004 BKN
012/022 BKN-OVC/TA 01/IC LGT-MDT RIME
035-060/RM WIND COMP HEAD 020 MH310 TAS 180.
```

LEVEL	ECHO INTENSITY	PRECIPITATION INTENSITY	POSSIBLE TURBULENCE	WIND GUSTS	HAIL	LIGHTNING
1	WEAK	LIGHT	LGT/MDT			
2	MODERATE	MODERATE	LGT/MDT			
3	STRONG	HEAVY	SEVERE			
4	VERY STRONG	VERY HEAVY	SEVERE	POSSIBLE	POSSIBLE	YES
5	INTENSE	INTENSE	SEVERE	ORGANIZED	LIKELY	YES
6	EXTREME	EXTREME	SEVERE	EXTENSIVE	LARGE	YES

* The numbers representing the intensity level do not appear on the chart. Beginning from the first contour line, bordering the area, the intensity level is 1-2; second contour is 3-4; and third contour is 5-6.

450

Highest precipitation tops in area in hundreds of feet.

SYMBOL	MEANING
R	RAIN
RW	RAIN SHOWERS
A	HAIL
S	SNOW
IP	ICE PELLETS
SW	SNOW SHOWERS
L	DRIZZLE
T	THUNDERSTORM
ZR, ZL	FREEZING PRECIPITATION
NE	NO ECHOES OBSERVED
NA	OBSERVATIONS UNAVAILABLE
OM	OUT FOR MAINTENANCE
STC	STC ON -- all precipitation may not be seen

SYMBOLS USED ON CHART

SYMBOL	MEANING
+	INTENSITY INCREASING OR NEW ECHO
-	INTENSITY DECREASING
NO SYMBOL	NO CHANGE
35	CELL MOVEMENT TO NE AT 35 KNOTS
→	LINE OR AREA MOVEMENT TO EAST AT 20 KNOTS
MA	ECHOES MOSTLY ALOFT
PA	ECHOES PARTLY ALOFT

SYMBOL	MEANING
	LINE OF ECHOES
SLD	OVER 9/10 COVERAGE IN A LINE
WS999	THUNDERSTORM WATCH
WT999	TORNADO WATCH
LEWP	LINE ECHO WAVE PATTERN

Fig. 7-8. Key to radar summary.

153

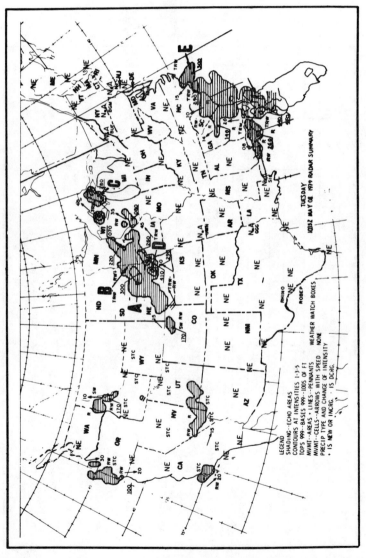

Fig. 7-9. Every pilot should check the radar summary for every flight.

left at the nine o'clock position of the reporting station's cycle. Visibilities are not included unless they are less than six miles. At the six o'clock position, the ceiling is given and the last zeroes are dropped. Fifteen would be 1,500 feet, and 250 would be 25,000 feet.

What cloud condition and visibility is indicated for southwestern Utah (b) on the 1600Z Weather Depiction Chart? (See Fig. 7-10.)

1. Scattered clouds ranging from 3000 to 6000 feet; visibility more than six miles.
2. Thin overcast from 3000 to 6000 feet; visibility unlimited.
3. A broken overcast ranging from 3000 to 6000 feet; visibility not reported.
4. Overcast 3000 to 6000; unlimited visibility below the overcast.

The circle is only one-fourth colored. That indicates only a scattered cloud layer. No visibility is printed at the nine o'clock position, so you must assume it is greater than six miles. Printed at the six o'clock position is the cloud base height. These read between 3000 and 6000. You must assume then, that choice No. 1 is the correct one.

Try another.

You are on the IFR flight from northeast Kansas (d) to southeast Colorado (c) and experience complete electrical failure. Based on the information shown on the Weather Depiction Chart (See Fig. 7-12), which would be your best escape route?

1. Fly northwest to Utah.
2. Reverse course and return to Kansas.
3. Fly south until VFR conditions are reached.
4. Continue your present heading until you reach an area of scattered clouds.

With such an interpretive question, a correct answer may be difficult to perceive. It appears to me, however, that the shortest route to VFR should be the way to go. Because the route to be flown borders on a marginal VFR depiction to the south, it appears that a deviation to the south would be quickest and least. I'd have to go with choice No. 3.

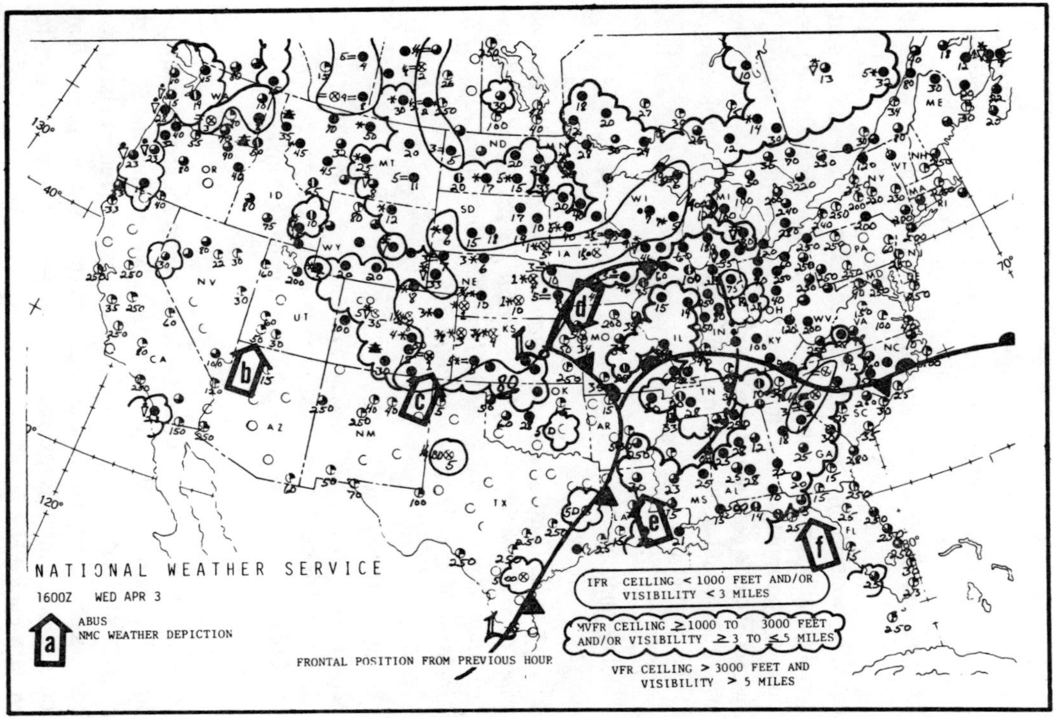

Fig. 7-10. The weather depiction chart shows a pilot at a glance where the weather is bad.

NATIONAL WEATHER SERVICE

WED APR 3
1600Z
ABUS
NMC WEATHER DEPICTION

FRONTAL POSITION FROM PREVIOUS HOUR

IFR CEILING < 1000 FEET AND/OR VISIBILITY < 3 MILES

MVFR CEILING ≥ 1000 TO 3000 FEET AND/OR VISIBILITY ≥ 3 TO ≤ 5 MILES

VFR CEILING > 3000 FEET AND VISIBILITY > 5 MILES

Figure 7-11 is an excerpt from a U. S. High Level Significant Prognostic Chart. It indicates . . .

1. continuous dense cirriform clouds covering five-eighths of the sky with bases and tops 24,000 ft. and 30,000 ft., respectively.
2. five layers of clouds with bases and tops 24,000 ft. and 30,000 ft., respectively.
3. five-tenths of the sky covered by layered clouds with cumulonimbus tops 30,000 ft.
4. 50 percent probability of layered cirriform clouds with tops ranging between 24,000 and 30,000 ft.

The symbol indicates that there is five-eighths coverage of clouds. The altitudes of 24,000 to 30,000 are the domain of cirriform clouds. Only thunderstorms protrude into this are of the atmosphere and no TRW is indicated. The answer is No. 1.

The Terminal Forecast is ready very much like the hourly sequence reports. Ceilings, however, are denoted by a C in front of the estimated number. The FT as they are called, begin with a code such as "MEM 251010." This code begins with the station identifier. The following six digits are the day of the month (25 in this example), and the valid zulu times; 10Z on the 25th until 10Z on the 26th day of the month. Let's examine a few terminal forecast questions to see how you do.

What is the latest time the FTWFT AMD1 is valid? (See Table 7-3.)

1. 1410Z, 26th day of the month.
2. 1425Z, 26th day of the month.
3. 1000Z, 26th day of the month.
4. 0400Z, 26th day of the month.

The FT for Fort Worth with amendment 1 is valid from 14Z on the 25th day of the month until 10Z on the 26th day of the month. Ordinarily, the forecasts cover a 24 hour period. This is an amendment though, and covers a lesser designated period chosen by the

Fig. 7-11. Cloud layers between 30,000 and 24,000 feet.

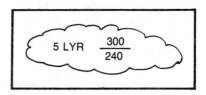

Table 7-3. Question Reference.

```
MEM 251010 C5 X 1/2S-BS 3325G35 OCNL CØ X ØS+BS.  16Z C3Ø BKN 3BS BRF SW-.  22Z 3Ø SCT 3315.
ØØZ CLR.  Ø4Z VFR WIND..


BUF FT RTD 251615 162ØZ 1ØØ SCT 25Ø SCT 181Ø.  18Z 5Ø SCT 1ØØ SCT 1913 CHC C3Ø BKN 3TRW AFT
2ØZ.  Ø3Z 1ØØ SCT C25Ø BKN.  Ø9Z VFR..


FTW FT AMD 1 25141Ø 1425Z C8 OVC 4F OVC V BKN.  15Z 2Ø SCT 25Ø-BKN.  19Z 4Ø SCT 12Ø SCT CHC
C3Ø BKN 3TRW.  Ø4Z MVFR CIG F..
```

NWS when they made the amendment. An interesting point here is that forecasts are amended. That makes a good case for in-flight weather briefings. Weather can and does change fast. The amendment could have been issued after your initial ground weather briefing. By the way, choice No. 3 is correct.

What conditions are forecast for FTW in the six-hour categorical outlook portion of the amended terminal forecast?

1. 4,000 scattered, 12,000 scattered.
2. Marginal VFR conditions with low ceilings and fog.
3. Chance of ceiling 3,000 broken with three miles visibility in thunderstorms.
4. 2,000 scattered, 25,000 thin broken; and after 1900Z, 4,000 scattered, 12,000 scattered with a chance of ceiling 3,000 broken, three miles visibility in thunderstorm.

What is a six-hour categorical outlook? That is the comment at the end of the terminal forecast. It is always six hours long ending at the last valid time. This one runs from 04Z to 10Z. The outlook is the marginal VFR ceilings and fog. The best choice is No. 2.

What condition is expected to cause the low visibility at MEM?

1. Lowering of ceiling to 0.
2. Gusty winds and blowing sand.
3. Smoke plus blowing sand.
4. Blowing snow.

Answer No. 4 is the correct choice.

In order to list Memphis as your alternate, your ETA at Memphis International can be no earlier than . . .

1. 1800Z.
2. 1600Z.
3. 2200Z.
4. 0000Z.

Here the FAA incorporates two questions into one. If you don't have the knowledge to answer both questions, then you will miss the question entirely. Returning to the FARs on flight planning and choosing an alternate, you must recall what time period the forecast for an alternate applies. A forecast for an alternate must apply at the estimated time of arrival only. Also, you have alternate minimums you must take into consideration. Those are, if you recall, "600-2" for a precision approach, and "800-2" for a nonprecision approach. Now that you have your weather minimums defined, you must look at the forecast and find the time period that the weather is expected to be above the alternate minimum. According to the MEM terminal forecast, the weather is to be 500 feet or lower until 16Z; therefore, 16Z is the earliest time you may use MEM as an alternate. Choice No. 2 is the correct choice.

It has been my experience that Flight Service personnel do not like to read the area forecast to a pilot. This may be because they feel it is not significant or too general. Its generality is where its beauty lies. The FA or area forecast is a great aid, because it describes the weather picture for an entire area. It is hard to get pilots to check the FA. They feel that if you get the hourly sequence at each end, and maybe one in the middle, plus a terminal forecast for the same, then they are covered. If a pilot knows what the fronts and lows are expected to do, an important inflight decision may be a great deal easier.

The way the FAA chooses the questions on area forecasts, makes them simple to answer. At the beginning of each paragraph on the forecast the subject area is defined. Usually, the FAA asks a question aimed at one of those paragraph headings. Example, the following question:

What is the outlook (17-19Z SAT) for the area north of the cold front? (See Table 7-4.)

1. Mostly VFR.
2. Variable, generally broken clouds.
3. Low visibility due to blowing dust.
4. Clear of clouds after frontal passage.

First, look for the paragraph heading "north of the cold front." Then, read and find an answer most like the choices. The answer is No. 2. You should have no problem answering these types of questions.

When is there a risk of encountering severe icing as outlines by the area forecast?

1. Anytime you fly above the freezing level.
2. Anytime you fly in the clouds.
3. When above freezing level and in precipitation.
4. Above 5,000 feet in the clouds.

Once again, you should look for a paragraph heading on icing. It is important here to be able to decipher the abbreviations. ICGIP stands for icing in precipitation. According to the forecast, you can expect severe icing in precipitation if you are above the freezing level. Answer No. 3 is correct.

Understanding the abbreviations in an area forecast is usually the hardest barrier to cross in interpreting them. A good textbook will be a great value here. The key to answering these questions properly is to look for the paragraph heading. You should not have too much trouble with these questions. And why not start using the FA in real flight situations if you don't already. Our tax money goes for the production and dissemination of these reports. Let's use them and be better prepared when snap inflight decisions arise.

The low level prognostic chart is a great help when planning flight a few days in advance or whenever a planned flight may be more than a one day trip. The low level prog charge is also displayed on the same sheet with a significant weather prognosis. It is divided into half by a vertical line. The two charts on the left side depict what the weather is believed to be 12 hours after data collection. It usually takes about three hours after the data is collected to disseminate these charts to other National Weather Service Stations and the network of Flight Service Stations. The chart, therefore, is not available until about nine hours before the valid time. The valid time is in the lower left-hand corner. The right-hand half of the chart is the low level prog chart and significant weather chart depicted as the weather is expected to appear 24 hours after the data collection.

On the low level prog chart, areas of precipitation are depicted. Solid lines indicate areas of continuous or intermittent precipita-

FA 121240
DFW FA 121240
13Z FRI-07Z SAT
OTLK 07Z-19Z SAT

NMEX OKLA TEX AND CSTL WTRS...

HGTS ASL UNLESS NOTED...

SYNS... LARGE INTNS LOW PRES AREA CNTRD OVR IA AT 13Z MOVG NEWD.   CDFNT ALG JLN TUL FSI PVW LVS
ALS LN AT 13Z MOVG SWD 25-30 KTS.

SIG CLDS AND WX....
CSTL WTRS... GENLY SCT CLDS 20-30 VRBL HI CI CLDS ABV.   OTLK...MVFR PSBL BRF LIFR TRW.

SE OF DRT BWD MLC FSM LN EXCP FOR THE CSTL WTRS... LN TSTMS ALG AUS DRT LN AT 13Z MOVG SEWD ABT
15 KTS AND DCRG BY 15Z. TSTMS REDVLPG OVR SRN AND ERN OK BY 18Z. CIGS ARND 10 VSBYS BLO 3 MIS
GUSTY SFC WNDS AND HAIL WITH CB TOPS TO 500 IN HVYR TSTMS.   OUTSIDE TSTMS VRBL CONDS GENLY CIGS
8-18 BUT LCLY CIGS AND VSBYS ZERO ZERO IN FOG AT 13Z. FOG DSIPTG CIGS IPVG TO ABV 20 BY 17Z.
CLRG AFT FROPA.   OTLK... MOSTLY VFR.

-N OF CDFNT... VRBL GENLY BKN CLDS CIGS 20-30. SFC WNDS OCNL 3625G45 WITH SOME DUST AND BLWG
DUST VSBYS OCNLY LWRG 2-6 MIS MAINLY OVR NWRN TEX AND WRN OKLA. SNW OCNL OBSCD MTNS OVR NMEX.
WNDS DCRG AFT DARK. COLDS DCRG BY 07Z.   OTLK... MOSTLY VFR.

ELSW... GENLY CLR EXCP IN MTN SECS OF NMEX OCNL 100-150 SCT TO OVC WITH SNW OCNL OBSCG HIR
MTNS TIL 00Z.   OTLK... MOSTLY VFR.

ICG... RISK ISOLD SVR ICGIP ABV FRZG LVL.   FRZG LVL SFC NRN OKLA NRN NMEX SLPG TO 140 OVR CSTL
WTRS.

Table 7-4. Area
Weather Forecast.

161

tion. Shaded areas are of five-tenths coverage or greater. Dotted lines are areas of showers. Any area not shaded is of less than five-tenths coverage. Let's check out a few questions using these charts.

What type precipitation is expected in Louisiana at 1800Z? (See Fig. 7-12.)

1. Rain showers over the entire area.
2. Rain showers and thunderstorms affecting five-tenths or more of the area.
3. Continuous rain in five-tenths or more of the area.
4. Continuous rain over the entire area.

The area across Louisiana on the VT1800Z chart is surrounded by a dotted line indicating showers. The inner portion between the dotted lines is shaded. This means the coverage is going to be five-tenths or greater. Therefore, answer No. 2 is the proper choice.

At what altitude is the freezing level in central Oklahoma as forecast on the 12-hour significant weather prog?

1. 4,000 feet.
2. 8,000 feet.
3. 400 feet.
4. 800 feet.

Checking the legend at the bottom of the significant weather prog chart, you will find the dotted line. The dotted line represents the freezing level above sea level. The height above sea level can be found at the left edge of the chart. It is 8,000 feet. Therefore, answer No. 3 is the correct choice.

A good weather briefing is as essential to conducting a safe flight as is the preflight walk-around inspection. Understanding how to use weather briefings is as much an art as is forecasting the weather itself. If you believe that a weather briefing is to find out if it's raining here and at the other end, then the sad truth will raise its ugly head someday. Instrument flying cannot support the average private pilot attitude of not needing to know the facts after getting by the written exam. Weather is more important than any other single issue of flight safety. You wouldn't take an inadequately fueled airplane cross country. Don't take an inadequately prepared brain either.

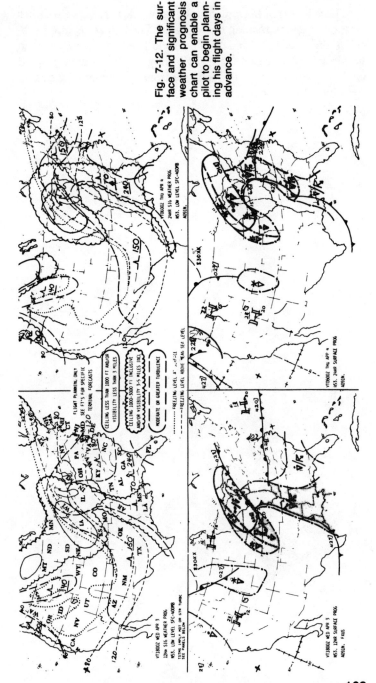

Fig. 7-12. The surface and significant weather prognosis chart can enable a pilot to begin planning his flight days in advance.

163

There have not been many innovative ideas to make weather questions easy by reading this chapter. The subject is more subjective then objective and does not lend itself to memory aids in the form I must present here. Following the tips I have pointed out, however, will make deductive reasoning a commodity easy to come by in the test room.

Chapter 8
Taking the Test

After weeks of study, hours of ground school, scores of questions to your instructor, you notice you begin to ask less questions. You are learning and retaining the information. At last, your instructor, now five inches shorter from you quizzing his legs off, signs his name and declares you competent to take the written test. He'll point you in the direction of the nearest GADO or FSS that gives the test. Most test offices are ready for testing about 8:30 A.M. That is when I recommend you show up. That will give you the maximum amount of time. It is possible to show up too late in the day and not have time to finish. In that case, the FAA would not even let you begin the test.

Upon arrival at the test facility you should have all of the things you need to present to the FAA. Below is a checklist that should be completed before leaving home.

PRE-TEST CHECKLIST

1. Flight instructor authorization to take the test, or evidence of completing a home study course.
2. Airman's Certificate and Medical
3. Flight Computer
4. Pocket Calculator (optional)
5. Formula Memory Sheet (not allowed in test room)

Several times in this book, I have mentioned the formula memory sheet. What is it? Well, it is a tried and true idea also developed by Bill Phelps Airline Ground Schools. Everyone has a photographic memory. Some of us don't know how to call upon it to aid us. But, the formula memory sheet, if drawn at least five times by hand, and studied five minutes just prior to entering the test facility, will be sufficient to ensure that you will have total recall in the test room.

The way the formula memory sheet (Fig. 8-1) works is to divide the sheet of paper (the FAA will provide ample scratch paper) into several divisions as shown. Each type of formula has its own space. It is important to study it at least five minutes just prior to entering the test facility. Once inside the test room, the first thing you should do *before* signing the test answer sheet is to write down the formulas. When you write the formula memory sheet in the test

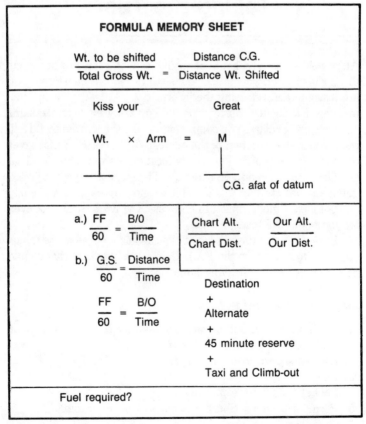

Fig. 8-1. The Formula Memory Sheet will aid you in taking the test.

room, begin by drawing the division lines. Then, like magic, the formulas will come to mind and you can just write them in the blank areas as fast as you can go. Remember, do it first thing in the test room.

QUESTION SELECTION SHEET

In this chapter, a sample question selection sheet and question answer sheet are included. Needless to say, care must be taken to correctly place your answer in the proper space. But, the greatest danger in taking the test is proper use of the question selection sheet. This sheet has a list of 80 questions selected at random by a computer. The fact that these questions are not consecutive numbers makes it easy for an applicant to answer the next consecutive question and not answer the correct question.

Examine the sample question selection sheet (Fig. 8-2). The first question to be answered is No. 4. In the normal scheme of things, you would probably go on to No. 5. That would be a mistake. The best way to use the selection sheet is to use a pencil and mark through both numbers as you finish the question. That will eliminate the chance for error on incorrect selection of questions.

Here are some other tips on actually taking the test. See Fig. 8- 3. The following points should be kept in mind while taking the test. One should answer test questions in accordance with the latest regulations and procedures. The test is continually updated. It is also important, obviously, to be sure that study material is also up to date.

Too many times, failure on the written exam is caused by not reading carefully rather than a lack of knowledge. Probably the most important test taking rule is R.T.F.Q. (read the friggin' question). Do not attempt to solve the question until you understand what it is asking. In other familiar words, "See the target clearly!"

The FAA maintains that there are no "trick" questions on the written exam. This is true. It is the author's belief, though, that there are some really tricky questions. I have already discussed many of these. Generally, these questions are direct quotes from regulations. The fact is that more than one answer choice may seem correct. This may cause a dilemma. In this case, you should pick the answer that seems best. If you know the regulations, however, the correct answer will be a direct quote.

The average time required to complete the test is four hours. Using the techniques described in this book, you may be able to better that considerably, but don't spend excessive time on ques-

QUESTION SELECTION SHEET

TITLE	SELECTION NO.
INSTRUMENT RATING – AIRPLANE	

NAME _____

NOTE: (1) IT IS PERMISSIBLE TO MARK ON THIS SHEET

(2) LEGEND MATERIAL IS IN QUESTION BOOK APPENDIX, PAGES 187 THROUGH 201

On Answer Sheet For Item No.	Answer Question Number	On Answer Sheet For Item No.	Answer Question Number	On Answer Sheet For Item No.	Answer Question Number	On Answer Sheet For Item No.	Answer Question Number
1	4	21	279	41	597	61	869
2	23	22	286	42	606	62	891
3	39	23	301	43	611	63	898
4	50	24	336	44	615	64	910
5	68	25	362	45	636	65	912
6	82	26	365	46	647	66	915
7	83	27	373	47	685	67	941
8	103	28	381	48	689	68	944
9	119	29	410	49	693	69	957
10	122	30	421	50	706	70	959
11	135	31	455	51	707	71	966
12	190	32	457	52	725	72	971
13	213	33	496	53	740	73	975
14	218	34	504	54	773	74	980
15	235	35	516	55	778	75	986
16	237	36	520	56	806	76	1002
17	253	37	524	57	822	77	1004
18	256	38	557	58	825	78	1007
19	266	39	577	59	840	79	1009
20	273	40	581	60	862	80	1013

BEFORE TURNING IN YOUR ANSWER SHEET, BE SURE THAT YOU HAVE COMPLIED WITH THE SPECIFIC INSTRUCTIONS ON PAGES 1 AND 4 OF THE AIRMAN WRITTEN TEST APPLICATION.

For Official Use Only

Fig. 8-2. A sample question selection sheet.

tions that stump you. You should go on to questions that can be answered readily and later return to the Question Selection Sheet for the questions that gave you trouble. Many times, you may find you just didn't R.T.F.Q. correctly upon returning to the question, and it becomes easy the second time around.

Computer problems generally take the largest part of your allotted time. Many times, the solution one arrives at is not exactly the same as what the FAA has available for answer choices. I indicated earlier in the book that the FAA uses various types of computers to check their solution. As a result, your answer may not be right on the money. The FAA says to choose the nearest answer to your solution. If your computations and methods are correct, you will inevitably choose the correct choice. Remember, on computer problems use the "plan of attack."

Many applicants, after completing all of the questions, go back through the test and double check their answers. This is probably

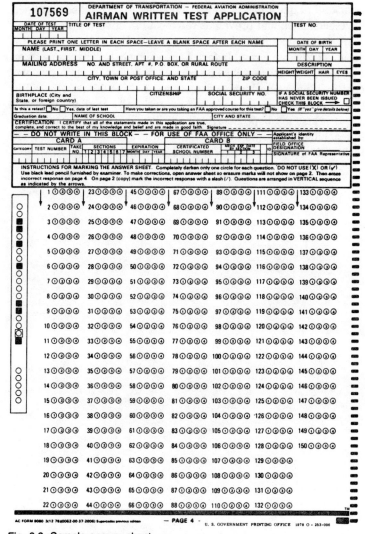

Fig. 8-3. Sample answer sheet.

an area of personal preference. I have found that going back and changing answers is not a good practice. Trust your first impressions of a question. After four hours of answering questions, your mind is not at its freshest. It is a bad time to return to questions that have been answered and are most likely correct.

Although not every possible type of question that you may receive on the exam has been discussed, the same rules apply to all. It is my hope that the guidelines set forth here will enable you to attack all of questions in a logical manner. The methods outlined have been tried and proven as the most effective for passing any FAA written examination. I have merely adopted them to the Instrument Written Exam. In fact, I am willing to bet that using these methods, your score will be 85 percent or higher. Eighty- five percent may not seem high, but most written results usually fall in the 70 percent bracket even for exceptionally studious persons.

It is also my hope that this book is a significant aid to others in teaching applicants to pass the written exam. I wish you good luck with the test and lots of good instrument flying.

Appendix

Abbreviations and Acronyms

The following listing is the acronyms and abbreviations used throughout this book.

ADF—Automatic Directional Finder—the radio navigation equipment in the aircraft.
AIM—Airman's Information Manual
ARTS III—Computerized radar depicting ground speed, altitude, and aircraft type.
ATC—Air Traffic Control
DH—Decision Height
DME—Distance Measuring Equipment
ETA—Estimated Time of Arrival
FAA—Federal Aviation Administration
FAF—Final Approach Fix
FAR—Federal Aviation Regulation
FBO—Fixed Base Operator
HIRL—High Intensity Runway Lights
IFR—Instrument Flight Rules
ILS—Instrument Landing System
LDA—Localizer type Directional Approach
LOC—Localizer
MDA—Minimum Descent Altitude
MEA—Minimum Enroute Altitude
MOCA—Minimum Obstruction Clearance Altitude

MSL—Feet above sea level

NDB—Nondirectional Beacon—the ground based radio navigation equipment used in conjunction with the ADF

NOS—National Ocean Survey

NWS—National Weather Service

OBS—Omnibearing Selector

PAR—Precision Apprach Radar

PT—Procedure Turn

RNAV—Area Navigation

SID—Standard Instrument Departure

STAR—Standard Terminal Arrival Route

TACAN—Tactical Air Navigation

VFR—Visual Flight Rules

VOR—Very High Frequency Omnirange

Index